This book is dedicated to:

The ever-dedicated families of the hostages,
The courageous soldiers of the IDF,
And our beloved State of Israel.

May God give His nation strength and bless it with peace,
And bring them home now!

Table of Contents

Introduction

Haskel Lookstein

How should we go on with our lives in the aftermath of the horrific pogrom perpetrated by Hamas on October 7th?

How can we conduct "business as usual" while tens of thousands of Israeli soldiers – our sisters and brothers – are risking their lives to protect the Jewish people and the Jewish State?

How can we live normal lives while hundreds of hostages – women, men, elderly, and babies – are trapped in tunnels in Gaza for over a year?

The answer is that we must strive to retain some degree of normal life, but, at the same time, we must be acutely aware of how *Am Yisrael* is suffering over there, while we are living our normal lives here.

And so, we need constant and poignant reminders to retain that awareness. Among those reminders for our community are the following:

1. We say *Avinu Malkeinu* in *shul* at *Shacharit* and *Mincha every day*, including *Shabbat* and *Yom Tov*.
2. We recite Psalm 121 at the end of every service *every day*.

3. We recite the prayer for the soldiers of Israel *each time* we read the Torah.
4. Remarkable women assemble in our Rohr Chapel *every weekday morning* in impressive numbers to recite Tehillim.
5. We have large cut-outs of the hostages in the Main Synagogue and in seats alongside the Holy Ark so that we cannot forget their plight.

The most powerful reminder and the most profound inspiration for awareness has been the weekly email message from our Rabbi, Chaim Steinmetz, in which he eloquently relates the terrible crisis of our time to the Parsha of the week. We are proud to present a collection of *Divrei Chaim* since October 7 as a reminder of the ongoing crisis of today and as inspiration for how we must continue to respond to that crisis in the future.

May the coming year bring victory to Israel, and then, *Shalom al Yisrael.*

Preface

At 8:15 on the morning of October 7th, there was a knock at my door. I found it strange; our building's staff would never bother us that early on a Saturday. Standing outside was my neighbor, with a very distressed look on his face. "There was an attack in Israel," he said. I acknowledged the news, and was getting ready to say goodbye; a terror attack in Israel is sadly not too uncommon. Seeing my reaction, he added that "it was a bad attack."

I paused, unsure what "bad" meant, still expecting to return to my regular pre-synagogue preparations. Then he explained that although no one yet knew the full extent of the attack, hundreds were dead. Right then, I completely stopped everything else I was doing and focused on Israel.

In a moment, everything had changed; for Israel, for the Jewish people, and for our community.

Like so many others, I was obsessed with the news, waking up in the middle of the night to check for updates. For the first few days, it was not completely clear if the State of Israel could survive if the West Bank exploded, and Hezbollah, Syria and Iran joined the attack. My heart was filled with worries and queries. What would happen to the Jewish world if Israel collapsed? What would I tell my children and my congregation if Israel disappeared? What would I tell myself?

On a daily basis, our hearts oscillated between grief, pride, hope, and every other possible emotion. It was an emotional struggle. Each week, as I wrote my weekly email d'var Torah, I brought those struggles to the words of the parsha; it was inspiring to see how familiar passages suddenly took on new meaning. An obscure passage about a conflict between Isaac and the Philistines looked very different after I realized that those age-old events had taken place less than a mile from the site of the Nova Festival. An unusual command about how to treat a poor litigant offered insights into the world's reaction to the attack. Timeless wisdom about the meaning of mourning became a required life lesson. The antisemitic storm unleashed by Hamas's willing collaborators around the world recalled a medieval lesson from Rashi's grandson.

As the year went on, these weekly emails became a chronicle of how the Torah offers renewed enlightenment in times of crisis. They are often a snapshot of the moment they were written; my moods, our moods, would fluctuate from week to week, and the assumptions of what might happen next were constantly changing. Certain themes and ideas were repeated; other times, I changed my mind as the year went on. But together these essays create a mosaic, a unified picture of a year when spirituality was both a struggle and a strength. For that reason, they are now being published together in this book.

I owe an enormous debt of gratitude to many people who made this book possible. David Suissa of the Jewish Journal has been an incredible friend and supporter, and has edited and published my weekly d'var Torah. His constant encouragement over the years has been invaluable. Each week, Riva Alper and Esther Feierman of our KJ team edit and set up my weekly email to the congregation. I am extremely grateful for their dedication and willingness to work at all hours in order to get the d'var Torah out on Thursday night. Ruthie Hollander's devotion to this project is truly a gift. She relentlessly encouraged me to put together this book, and both designed it and got it published. I am blessed to have a wonderful group of colleagues at Kehilath Jeshurun, as well as a remarkable lay leadership who are always ready to serve the Jewish people without reservation. In particular I need to acknowledge our Rabbi Emeritus, Haskel Lookstein, who is an inspiration and role model for what *ahavat yisrael* means; his example has guided me throughout my years at KJ, but in particular in the past year. I thank him as well for the enormous kindness of writing the foreword to this book.

Our children Akiva, Hillel, Eitan, and Ilana are the greatest blessings of our lives; and I am so proud of their dedication to Israel and Judaism, the very themes of this book. And *acharon acharon chavivah*: my dear wife Lisa has always been there for me, always supported me, and has always been at my side during our rabbinic journey. I am so lucky to share my life with her.

May the new year of 5785 be filled with blessing, and bring us healing and hope.

Despite the Tears, A Shehecheyanu

Bereishit / October 13

There are times when the grief-stricken must recite a Shehecheyanu.

This blessing is meant for joyous occasions, and thanks God for having "kept us alive, sustained us, and brought us to this moment."

When one is grieving, this blessing seems out of place. But Jewish law expects mourners to recite this blessing when they are the beneficiaries of a gift. We don't ignore the good, even in the worst circumstances.

This past week, I was thinking about a Shehecheyanu that was recited 80 years ago.

In *Hasidic Tales of the Holocaust*, Yaffa Eliach recounts when the Bluzhever Rebbe, Rabbi Israel Spira, recited this blessing on a Chanukah evening in the Bergen Belsen Concentration Camp, while lighting the Menorah:

> "....a wooden clog, the shoe of one of the inmates, became a hanukkiah; strings pulled from a concentration camp uniform, a wick; and the black camp shoe polish, oil.
>
> Not far from the heaps of the bodies, the living skeletons assembled to participate in the kindling of Hanukkah lights.

The Rabbi of Bluzhov lit the first light and chanted the first two blessings...When he was about to recite the third blessing, he stopped, turned his head, and looked around as if he were searching for something.

Immediately, he turned his face back to the quivering small lights and in a strong, reassuring, comforting voice, chanted the third, Shehecheyanu blessing: "Blessed art Thou, O Lord our God, King of the Universe, who has kept us alive, sustained us, and brought us to this moment."

Among the people present at the kindling of the lights was Mr. Zamietchkowski, one of the leaders of the Warsaw Bund... Afterward, he turned to the rabbi and said, "I can understand your need to light Hanukkah candles in these wretched times. I can even understand the historical note of the second blessing, 'Who brought miracles for our fathers in days of old, at this season.' But the fact that you recited the third blessing is beyond me. How could you thank God and say 'Blessed art Thou, O Lord our God, who has kept us alive, sustained us, and brought us to this moment'? How could you say it when hundreds of dead Jewish bodies are literally lying within the shadows of the Hanukkah lights ...and millions more are being massacred? For this you are thankful to God? For this you praise the Lord? This you call 'keeping us alive'?"

"Zamietchkowski, you are a hundred percent right," answered the rabbi. "When I reached the third blessing, I also hesitated and asked myself, what should I do with this blessing? ... But as I turned my head, I noticed that behind me a throng was standing, a large crowd of living Jews, their faces expressing faith and devotion... I said to myself, if God, blessed be He, has such a nation that at times like these ... stand and ... listen to the Hanukkah blessing, ... if, indeed, I was blessed to see such a people with so much faith and fervor, then I am under a special obligation to recite the third blessing.""

What the Bluzhever Rebbe said then is particularly relevant now, as we search for hope while engulfed by tragedy.

Yes, our grief is overwhelming. A friend of mine in Israel told me that his children who serve in the IDF have lost more friends in the past few days than he did in his lifetime. Entire families have been wiped out. The loss is so severe that Israeli cemeteries are calling for volunteers to dig graves. The Jewish people are in mourning, no more than two degrees of separation from someone who was murdered or kidnapped.

Analogies fail when it comes to this attack. To call it a pogrom is a dramatic understatement. Even 9/11, which remains a deep American trauma 22 years later, pales in comparison to this attack; the Simchat Torah massacre is the equivalent of thirteen 9/11s. The only possible analogy for the two days of horror is the Holocaust.

The barbarism of Hamas is incomprehensible. They murdered individuals by shooting them at point-blank range with rocket-propelled grenades. They slit throats. They massacred 40 babies. They took such pride in their depravity that they videotaped what they did.

Actually, "incomprehensible" is the wrong word to describe Hamas's crimes. Good people simply have a failure of imagination, unable to understand the mindset of those who are evil. And that is a flaw. It hobbles democracies when they have to take on dictatorships; they imagine they can negotiate with those who are ruthless and "bring out the best" in them. One who desires love finds it difficult to imagine that there are people who have a passion for cruelty.

Our Torah reading introduces us to Lemech, the first person who takes joy in violence. He boastfully recites the following poem to his wives:

> "For I have killed a man as soon as I wounded him,
> Even a young man as soon as I hurt him.
> If Cain shall be avenged sevenfold,
> Then Lamech seventy-sevenfold."

This passage is enigmatic and difficult to interpret, and commentators offer multiple approaches. But the above translation is based on the commentary of Umberto Cassuto, who follows the approach of Rabbeinu Bachya. Lemech is the one who popularizes violence; his son is the inventor of the sword. Lemech sings about how strong he is, how easily he killed a young boy who displeased him; as Cassuto puts it, Lemech "boasts with great bravado of this cruel murder."

There are always people who love violence. Lemech and his son Tubal-Cain refine the brutality of their ancestor Cain. While most people compose songs of love and inspiration, Lemech sings a song of death. And the Torah wants to show us, up close, that there are evil human beings like Lemech in this world.

It is fascinating that Lemech refers to God's protection of Cain. This reminds us that forgiveness is not endless. Perhaps Cain deserved God's mercy; he had committed a then-unfamiliar crime and did so in extreme jealousy. But Lemech mocks God's kindness towards Cain by expecting the same for himself. This violent murderer has the brazen chutzpah to demand forgiveness afterward.

What Hamas and its helpers in the international community do is pretty much the same. They expect all of their brutal crimes to be completely forgiven and any mistake by Israel to be severely punished. Our dear member Gilad Erdan has to combat the endless lies disseminated in the United Nations; there, dictatorships that murder their own people make speeches excoriating Israel, and everyone listens intently to their prattling propaganda. But Hamas's constant lying shouldn't surprise us; if one is willing to murder babies, how difficult is it to lie?

For the tragedies of this past week we all weep, and our eyes flow with tears. Yet even so, we must make a Shehecheyanu, just like the Bluzhever Rebbe eighty years ago.

We must make a Shehecheyanu on exceptional kindness. A friend described what is happening in

Israel as a "balagan of *chesed*," or a chaotic whirlwind of kindness. Everywhere people are running everywhere to do what they can for those in need. One Chabad in Jerusalem packed 25,000 sandwiches for the soldiers. There are hours-long waits at hospitals to donate blood because so many people have come forward. Hundreds of volunteers have come to Siroka Hospital to help the wounded and their families with laundry, prescriptions, and rides. And here in New York, a lone man stood inside Kennedy Airport, buying plane tickets for soldiers returning home.

We have to make a Shehecheyanu on the beautiful unity. This was not the case at all a few weeks ago; but now, in a crisis, Israel has once again pulled together. Yotam and Assaf Doctor, who own the aptly named "Brothers Restaurant" in Tel Aviv, started delivering thousands of meals to the front lines. But many soldiers wouldn't eat them, because the restaurant wasn't kosher. What did the Doctor brothers do? They called in the Rabbinate, and for the first time, became a kosher restaurant. The Jewish people are brothers and sisters—and family must stick together, in good times and in bad.

We have to make a Shehecheyanu because of extraordinary courage. Perhaps, as the Haggadah says, in every generation someone comes to destroy the Jewish people. But more important to remember is that in every generation we have found the courage to overcome those enemies. They have been tossed into the ash-heap of history, and we are still here.

This brings me to another Shehecheyanu story, from just a few days ago. Israeli media shared a video of David, a soldier in camouflage netting, holding his smartphone. David was participating in his son's bris, and saying his blessings while in the field of battle. Following the Sephardic tradition, David recited the Shehecheyanu blessing.

A pessimist might object to his Shehecheyanu, and see this as a moment of extreme disappointment. A young father should be with his family, not on the front lines endangering his life. A young mother should have her husband at her side, rather than worrying about whether he will ever get to hold his baby boy.

Even so, David's Shehecheyanu is a meaningful blessing, and expresses the destiny of the Jewish people. For much of Jewish history, we were defenseless. That ended with the establishment of the State of Israel. That's why, despite the circumstances, David can say Shehecheyanu.

At the end of the bris, David and his fellow soldiers recited the words from Ezekiel, "And I said to you in your blood you shall live, and I said to you in your blood you shall live." Some of the soldiers began to cry. It is a time of bloodshed; these soldiers have witnessed the aftermath of Hamas's atrocities. But the message of Ezekiel is that even in the worst times, Jews know that there will be better days ahead. Even amidst the blood, there shall be new life.

And for that, we can all make a Shehecheyanu.

We Will Rebuild, Even After This

Noach / October 20

Jewish history is an absurdity. How can a tiny nation persevere despite centuries of persecution? This question has been posed many times. Mark Twain wrote the following in an essay for *Harper's Magazine* in 1898: "All things are mortal but the Jew; all other forces pass, but he remains. What is the secret of his immortality?"

Many countries mastered empire-building. Twain lists the empires that once dominated the world but have since shriveled away: the Egyptians, the Babylonians, the Persians, the Greeks, and the Romans. They had dominating militaries and well-developed economies. But once these empires fell apart, they couldn't rebuild.

On the other hand, Jews have always known how to overcome adversity. The Yiddish phrase *"mir zaynen du"* (we are here) is both a description of Jewish history as well as the vow of Jewish determination.

After the barbaric Simchat Torah Massacre, we have once again seen Jewish determination in action. Israelis have come together to fight for their country, and the Jewish world has stood in solidarity with their brothers and sisters in Israel. Rabbi Joe Wolfson in Tel Aviv described it this way: "I have lived 100 years in 5 days. If there is one thing I know it's this. If we are like this we are truly undefeatable."

This courageous response is far from instinctive. Grief is an all-encompassing emotion. The darkness felt after experiencing trauma seems to lead in only one direction: resignation.

Comfort seems unattainable at such times. And this is what happens to Noah. After the flood, after the entire world is wiped out before his eyes, Noah immediately plants a vineyard and drinks its wine. George Bernard Shaw once remarked, "Alcohol is the anesthetic which enables the bereft man to endure the painful operation of living." Noah is simply searching for a way to numb the pain.

Another Biblical character, Lot, does much the same. After witnessing the destruction of Sodom, including the loss of several family members, he too turns to the bottle and gets drunk.

At first glance, their response is reasonable. The Talmud remarks that "wine was only created in order to comfort mourners." Noah and Lot are mourners searching for a way to cope with the pain.

Yet the Torah's verdict on their drinking is negative. Noah falls into a stupor and lies naked in clear sight of his children; he is later humiliated by his son and grandson. Lot, when he gets drunk, is seduced by his daughters. The outcome of these Biblical episodes is meant as an editorial comment; Noah and Lot's drinking is implicitly condemned.

But the question remains: What did they do wrong? Didn't the Talmud say that is what wine is for?

The answer can be found in a Midrash. It quotes the verse that says "Noah, a man of the soil, began to plant a vineyard," and comments: "Noah, a man of the soil, began [vayachel] – he lost his holiness and became ordinary [chullin]."

Using a play on the Hebrew word "vayachel", the Midrash deems Noah's behavior as merely ordinary, rather than holy (e.g., the word in the Talmud for ordinary meat that isn't from a sacrifice, "chullin", comes from the same root). This itself is a bit puzzling. Generally, kohanim (priests) are considered to be uniquely holy because they are dedicated by God to the Temple service. But why would Noah be considered holy?

But that is exactly the point. Kohanim are prohibited from drinking when they are on call to serve in the Temple; they must be fully focused on their divine service. And like the kohanim, this Midrash argues that Noah also had a divine mission.

Noah's failure is that he didn't realize this. Another Midrash criticizes Noah for not wanting to leave the ark. Perhaps for an ordinary person, that would be completely understandable; who would want to go out and witness the destruction the flood left behind?

But more is demanded of Noah. If God selected him to be the only survivor of the flood, that means that Noah is being designated for the mission of rebuilding the world. He must not hide in the ark; like a kohen, he must remain focused on his mission. Noah must go out and rebuild the world. He has no time to get drunk and distracted.

The Midrash concludes by saying: "'And he planted a vineyard.' Should Noah not have planted something else that was constructive, perhaps a fig tree branch or an olive tree branch? Instead, 'he planted a vineyard.'"

Noah missed his calling.

Jews see rebuilding as sacred. In the previous generation, many of the Holocaust survivors, broken in both body and soul, saw their mission as rebuilding what was destroyed. They fought to create the State of Israel, established Jewish communities, schools, and synagogues, and built beautiful Jewish families.

Here, one can find the elusive secret of Jewish survival: the determination to rebuild.

This belief in rebuilding is part of Israel's DNA. Even during the worst days of the intifada, Israel moved forward. Greg Myre and Jennifer Griffin, two journalists who lived in Israel between 2000-2007, wrote that:

We were consistently amazed at how quickly Israelis returned to places that had been bombed. The police, the rescue teams, and the cleanup crews restored a bomb site to an outward semblance of normality within hours of an attack. Debris was swept out. Hoses washed away blood from the sidewalk. Shattered windows were replaced. The yellow police tape came down..... For Israelis, combating terror is not just a security question. It's a social, cultural, and psychological issue and the whole country is required to play its role. It's often measured in small deeds, like going back to a favorite cafe after an attack.

One must never allow destruction to be the final chapter.

Israel today is filled with grief, anxiety, and heartbreak. A cartoon now circulating shows a caricature of the map of Israel lying on the couch, while Sigmund Freud listens. The caption reads: "How does one find a psychologist for 9.3 million people?" So many families have experienced horrific loss; the families of hostages sit helplessly as their loved ones are held by a group of depraved murderers. Every Israeli, and every Jew, is heartbroken.

Even so, Israel is rebuilding. In Kibbutz Be'eri, where Hamas destroyed dozens of homes and murdered over 100 people, the famous printing house, which is the largest business in the area, has reopened. The surviving children, who are now housed in a hotel in the center of Israel, once again have a kindergarten in their hotel. Photos posted online look pretty ordinary: toys, books, cheery signs, and sippy cups with each child's name. Yet that kindergarten is quite extraordinary.

The weddings are also extraordinary. The Talmud says that every rejoicing bride and groom is the equivalent of rebuilding one of the destroyed buildings of Jerusalem; and today in Israel, young couples are coming forward to take part in the heroic act of Jewish rebuilding.

Tamar and Adir had not yet made plans to get married. But once the war broke out, they decided it was time; the future could no longer wait. They had a joyous wedding near the front and walked down the aisle in their military uniforms. The video of them dancing with their parents into the Chuppah has gone viral in Israel. There are so many weddings of this kind that one newspaper wrote an article about all of the "Weddings Under Fire."

Total strangers have come forward to help with these celebrations. Aviva and Yisrael, one of the engaged couples that moved up their wedding date, had decided to have a simple affair; their family, who lived in the South, couldn't leave their homes to attend. They asked a local rabbi to help with a minyan for the wedding. The Rabbi shared the request on social media.

Aviva explains what happened next: "Two amazing guys from Ramot, Naveh, and Ori, stepped in and helped organize everything. A hall, food, a photographer, musicians, and a DJ all materialized seemingly from thin air—the goodwill of Jewish people wishing to celebrate with a brother and sister they'd never met."

Every wedding is another step towards a better future. The Jewish tradition encourages the brokenhearted to find the inner strength to marry, have babies, and build communities, even after they have experienced death and destruction. The Jewish way forward is the way of rebuilding. And that has been the secret of Jewish survival.

We are all uncertain what will happen in the next few months. But one thing is certain: Israel will rebuild. Jews have always been ready to write the next chapter of Jewish History.

Am Yisrael Chai!

Our Family Has Arrived

Lech Lecha / October 26

"*Avram haIvri*" is a curious term; the word "*Ivri*" is most often associated with Egypt, and first used in our Torah reading. The meaning of this word is also unclear. But one interpretation in the Midrash is frequently quoted. Rabbi Judah interprets "*Ivri*" as meaning "the entire world was on one side and Abraham was on the other ("*m'ever*") side." He sees in this phrase a critical aspect of Abraham's mission: to stand apart from the rest of the world. Jews are meant to remain eternal iconoclasts, beginning with the rejection of idolatry.

To live apart need not mean living alone. Abraham himself had close allies; Mamre, Eshkol, and Aner are mentioned in the very same verse as having formed a covenant with Abraham. There were people then, as now, who appreciated the Jews for their differences, not just despite them.

These allies are exceptionally important now. As I traveled through Israel this week, Israelis of every political persuasion told me how grateful they were for the stalwart support, both military and diplomatic, that the United States and President Biden have offered to Israel during this war. And it is not just the United States; England, France and Germany, among others, have come forward in support. Israel is not alone. Abraham would have found it difficult to fight his war against the four kings without the support of his allies; the same is true of Israel today.

Even so, living apart has had a profound impact on our history. The stubborn Jewish insistence on being a nation that dwells alone drew derision from the Greeks and fury from the Romans. Jewish rejection of Christianity and Islam provoked further animosity.

Over the centuries these negative attitudes slowly morphed into antisemitism, an amalgam of conspiracies that made the Jew the protagonist of all the world's ills.

Antisemitism has also shaped how Jews see themselves. It placed Jews under a microscope, with the behavior of any Jew becoming the standard by which every Jew is judged. Jews policed their own communities to ensure that no one antagonized the non-Jews.

The legacy of this endures. After being granted political rights, many Jews made sure to carefully modify their behavior to become more acceptable, cutting off their Jewish legs to fit the too short bed of "tolerance" a hostile world offered them. Jews imitated the very people who ridiculed them.

Among non-Jews, the constant and careful examination of Jews to see if they are actually worthy of being treated as equals became a stealth form of antisemitism, an expression of disgust hidden under the mask of "honest criticism." Every Jewish criminal was highlighted, and every Jewish misdeed exaggerated.

Both of these responses are on full display during this conflict. Jewish students who desperately want acceptance avoid expressing public support for Israel; a small group of them have become her fiercest critics. It is a Jewish Stockholm Syndrome, an unhealthy need to identify with those who detest you.

At the same time, Jewish students watch their friends rush out and protest on behalf of Hamas, even before Israel responded. These students feel profoundly betrayed by classmates and teachers who celebrate the murders of their fellow Jews.

The one-sided perspective of "honest criticism" of Jews leads to this. A monstrous massacre of burning, beheading, raping and kidnapping is quickly ignored and put on the back burner. At the same time, Israel's missteps are immediately seized upon. If Israel is thought to have bombed a hospital, the world is up in arms. When it turns out that Islamic Jihad actually bombed the hospital, the very same Palestinian deaths are no longer worth discussing.

It's lonely to be a Jew right now.

Another aspect of Jewish identity is also found in this week's parsha: a deep loyalty to family.

The Torah speaks at length about Abraham's war. Four kings come from the East to Canaan, to reassert their control over five local kings. Abraham rushes to defend the local kings.

One has to wonder why this is included in the Torah's account. Is it to show that Abraham is a capable General? Is it because he felt deeply connected to the local nations?

The answer is offered by the way the Torah phrases how Abraham heard the news; it says "and Abram heard that his brother was taken captive." Lot, Abraham's nephew, was taken captive during the war; Abraham is rushing to set him free. The Torah calls Lot Abraham's brother, even though he's actually his nephew, because it is speaking about Abraham's perspective: He loves Lot like a brother. And Abraham will do anything for his brother.

Abraham's war to free Lot is the first example in Jewish literature of what the rabbinic tradition calls "*pidyon shevuyim*", the ransoming of captives. Charity must be raised to ransom any Jew, even a complete stranger; pidyon shevuyim is considered by the Talmud to be the highest form of charity. No Jew can be left behind.

The Jewish passion for ransoming captives became so large that the Talmud had to insist that no ransom exceed the normal price one would pay for a slave; they didn't want kidnappers to consider

Jews lucrative targets. What is fascinating is that despite this ruling, over the centuries Jews continued to pay large ransoms, and developed halakhic rationales to allow it. The Jewish people consider themselves to be one large family; and like Abraham, could never turn away from a brother in need.

I was in Israel this past week with Rabbi Josh Lookstein representing our community. What we spoke about over and over with the people there is this bond of family. Israelis I met were moved to hear all our community has been doing on behalf of Israel at this time.

Everywhere, the metaphor of family came up; the remarkable organizations that have sprouted up everywhere to help the soldiers and the displaced are a reflection of this idea.

In Ichilov Hospital, I met a young man, Omer, who escaped the terrorists at Nova Festival, and was rescued because someone with him messaged a friend, who then drove down south to save them. I was told that this story was not unique; multiple people, after getting a text, jumped into their cars to help family and friends.

One such story, which has been reported widely, is about the Tibon family. Amir and Miri Tibon and their two little daughters live in Nachal Oz. They entered their safe room after hearing the sirens; a little while later they heard gunshots, and Amir immediately understood there were terrorists in the Kibbutz. He immediately texted his father Noam, a retired general, that Nachal Oz had been invaded. His father wrote back: "I'm coming."

Noam drove south. Much happened to Noam along the way, including a firefight with Hamas terrorists and transporting wounded soldiers. It took a lot of time. Noam finally met up with another retired general, and together they drove to Nachal Oz. There, they joined forces with a small group of soldiers who were getting ready to liberate the Kibbutz.

Meanwhile, inside the safe room, the two young girls were barely able to remain quiet. But Amir told them not to worry; that their grandfather, *Saba*, was coming. They just had to stay quiet a little longer.

Finally, after fighting the terrorists, Noam made his way to the house. He knocked on the window of the safe room and shouted, "I'm here." Hearing their grandfather's voice, the two little girls jumped up and shouted: "*Saba Higiyah*—grandfather has arrived."

I have thought about this story throughout the last two weeks. Family shows up when their relatives are in need. I can tell you that Israel's needs are enormous, economically, militarily, and emotionally. This is the greatest crisis since the Yom

Kippur War, and even greater than that as well. Before I went, I had monitored the news constantly. I imagined then that I had a good picture of what was happening, but now I realize that things are even more desperate than I thought.

I know our community has done so much already. But this is going to be a long journey, and we must not quit. We will need to give more, lobby more, demonstrate more, and just do more of everything.

Because when family needs you, no distance is too long.

Just ask Noam.

Still a Despised Stranger, Still Standing Strong

Chayei Sara / November 10

The Biblical phrase "a stranger and a resident" is fraught with meaning for the modern Jew. Rabbi Joseph Soloveitchik points out that this phrase is self-contradictory, and asks: "How can one be a stranger and a resident at the same time?"

He explains that:

> Abraham's definition of his dual status... describes with profound accuracy the historical position of the Jew who resides in a predominantly non-Jewish society. He was a resident, ...sharing with them a concern for the welfare of society, and contributing to the progress of the country in loyalty to its government and institutions. ....However, there was another aspect, the spiritual, in which Abraham regarded himself as a stranger. His identification and solidarity with his fellow citizens....did not imply his readiness to relinquish any aspects of his religious uniqueness. His was a different faith ... which set him apart from the larger faith community.

Soloveitchik reads the words "a stranger and a resident" poetically, seeing this paradoxical phrase as a reflection of the dual commitment that Modern Orthodox American Jews make: to be both a loyal citizen and a devoted Jew at the same time. He sees the challenge for American Jews as being how to fully embrace their country and culture without assimilating away any of their spiritual identity.

However, a closer look at the text offers a different interpretation. This unusual phrase has to be seen in context. Abraham describes himself as "a stranger and a resident" when he petitions the local Hittites in the hope of acquiring a permanent family burial ground. Abraham is worried the Hittites might reject his request because he is a stranger, so he assures them he plans on taking up permanent residence, and make their community his community. In other words, Abraham is turning to the Hittites and saying: will you accept me, the stranger, as a citizen?

It turns out that not only did the Hittites accept Abraham, but they honored him as a spiritual leader. Abraham the wanderer and outsider is finally embraced. He is a stranger no more.

Read this way, the text is a harbinger of the history of the Jews in America. Jews faced many challenges during their 370 years here, but eventually the Jews were accepted, and no longer needed to see themselves as both "a stranger and a resident." At least until recently.

There was a golden age, not too long ago, when Jews felt completely accepted in the United States. Had you asked me 15 years ago, I would have told you that combating antisemitism was a waste of communal money; Jew-hatred was a thing of the past, not a challenge of the future. But I was wrong, very wrong.

Antisemitism has grown, year after year; and it reached a crescendo on October 7th. The Hamas attack has unleashed unprecedented hatred of Jews.

The American Jewish world has been left in shock. We discovered that we are still strangers after all these years.

Part of it has to do with a misapprehension about antisemitism. Many people assume that antisemitism is just another variety of xenophobia, and the hatred of Jews is much like the hatred of every other minority group. This is partially correct. The Book of Esther does say that Haman demands the Jews be destroyed because their "customs are different from any other people." Xenophobia is as old as humanity itself.

Jews have also assumed that antisemitism is mere xenophobia, and so they endeavored mightily to prove to the world that they are no different than others. During World War I, German Jews volunteered for the army in disproportionate numbers, eager to shed the accusation they were cowardly and unpatriotic; 12,000 German Jews died on the battlefield. (Unfortunately, this didn't help; Jews were slandered as disloyal cowards anyway. And a few short years later, Germany elected Hitler.)

At times, Jews policed the behavior of other Jews in the hope of diminishing xenophobia. In the late 1800s and early 1900s, German Jews looked down on *Ostjuden*, the Jews from the East, who dressed differently, didn't speak the vernacular, and lacked German refinement. This form of social pressure was not unique to Germany; in post-war America, many felt that the oddly dressed Chasidic Jews prevented the acceptance of other Jews.

But this misses the point. Jew-hatred has raged in countries where no Jews live; at other times it has exploded in countries where Jews assimilated and blended in. David Nirenberg, in his book *Anti-Judaism*, points out that antisemitism often has a mythical quality, in which Judaism is cast as the polar opposite of one's beliefs, the very definition of what one isn't.

This type of antisemitism is often ideological. Medieval Christians didn't just see Judaism as a competing religion; Judaism was seen as containing noxious beliefs that could corrupt the soul. One need not be Jewish to be a victim of this type of anti-Judaism; in post-Expulsion Spain, Christian thinkers would often malign each other as being "Jewish" for having the wrong ideas, even though the country had no Jews left. For Communists, Jews were predatory capitalists; for Fascists, Jews were the vanguard of Communism. Judaism became the deviant philosophy against which everyone contrasted their "true" beliefs.

At the end of his book, which was published in 2013, Nirenberg writes, "We live in an age in which millions of people are exposed daily to some variant of the argument that the challenges of the world they live in are best explained in terms of Israel."

This reality was already evident then; it is ubiquitous now. Israel has, to borrow Jacob Talmon's phrase, become "the Jew among the nations," the devil which defines what deviance is.

Anti-Zionism is an ideology; and, like most ideologies, it is disseminated by the intelligentsia. The hatred for Israel that is roaring through college campuses is founded on the belief that Israel is the ultimate colonial state, the very incarnation of centuries of Western racism and exploitation. Considering Israel the echt-colonial state may seem absurd to anyone well versed in 3,800 years of Jewish history in the Holy Land. But such is the reality of myths; they need no reality. This new form of anti-Judaism means that the plight of the Palestinians is looked at with a microscope, while what happens to the Rohingyas or the Uighurs is barely worth anyone's attention. Like many other ideologies, anti-Zionism is dogmatic and uncompromising; the thought of offering any sympathy for kidnapped Israelis is beyond the pale.

One can reasonably discuss how, on the margins, anti-Zionism and antisemitism are not fully identical. But without a doubt, the myths that drive contemporary anti-Zionism are one and the same as the myths that lie behind antisemitism. And as we have seen over and over again, even the most carefully crafted protestations of anti-Zionism rapidly morph into antisemitism. This is what is happening on college campus after college campus, where harassment of Jewish students is an everyday event, and death threats and assaults are becoming too common an occurrence.

Jewish students are feeling betrayed. They can't believe that their own friends rushed out immediately on October 8th to show solidarity with the murderers of their brothers and sisters in Israel. And this betrayal goes all the way to the top, nurtured by professors and enabled by administrators.

This betrayal is not just a betrayal of Jewish college students; it is a betrayal of the American Jewish dream. After Jews immigrated to this country, it was at these very same universities that they found the tools to achieve success. The children of Jewish strangers from Europe and the Middle East were able to enter the mainstream of American life due to these universities. Just a few decades ago, these campuses were where Jews shed their past as strangers.

Now that's no longer true. On October 7th, American Jews woke up to find out that they are strangers once again.

Many Jews feel alienated right now, out of place in their workplaces, universities, and even in their favorite coffee shops. Like Abraham, Jews are once again wondering if they still belong.

But the story doesn't end here. What is remarkable is how many Jews have gotten involved in supporting Israel and combating antisemitism. Young and old, they organize dinners at Hillels and candlelight vigils at City Hall; they march on Washington and deliver supplies to Israel. They stand up for Israel and stand against antisemitism. Unlike Abraham, these Jews won't ask for acceptance; they will demand it.

And no one is going to tell them they don't belong.

The Magic of the Twice-Dug Well
Toldot / November 17

Where was Gerar located? Determining the location of biblical cities requires careful evaluation of archeological, historical, and literary evidence. It is both an art and a science, and consequently opens the door for multiple opinions.

Several archaeological sites, or "Tels," have been identified as Gerar. Eliezer Oren of Ben Gurion University has argued that Tel Haror, located between Ofakim and Netivot, is Gerar. It is a large city, and the location also seems to correspond to an ambiguous description given by the Church Father Eusebius in the 4th century.

Many other archeologists and Bible scholars take a different view. In the 1920s W. J. Phythian-Adams and Flinders Petrie identified the excavations at Tel Jemmeh with Gerar. They did so because a Byzantine village, Umm Gerar, with essentially the same name, was located nearby.

Yehuda and Yoel Elitzur, father and son Bible scholars, note that the biblical record corresponds with this identification. Gerar is described in the Tanakh as being close to Gaza, which is true of Tel Jemmeh but not of Tel Haror. Tel Jemmeh also is a place of abundant well water, which is characteristic of cities closer to the coast. A place like this is somewhere that one would naturally go to during a famine. Tel Jemmeh best fits the biblical description of Gerar.

Gerar's location was just a matter of academic interest until a month and a half ago; now, it is part of the geography of tragedy. The area of Tel Jemmeh is about a mile from Re'im, where the Nova Festival took place and 364 people were murdered. It is also very close to many of the Kibbutzim that were destroyed during the horrific, depraved Hamas massacre. Gerar is in the zone of tragedy; and now, after October 7th, this text speaks to us with a different voice.

Genesis 26 begins with Rebecca and Isaac leaving home in search of food during a famine. They arrive in Gerar on their way down to Egypt, but God tells them to stay there and not leave the Land of Israel.

In Gerar, they become extremely successful, to the point that the local people are jealous. The Philistines close up all of the wells in Gerar that Abraham had dug; Abimelech the local king tells Isaac: "Go away from us, for you have become far too big for us."

And so Isaac moves into the Valley of Gerar, and there "Isaac dug again the wells of water which they had dug in the days of Abraham his father (for the Philistines had stopped them up after the death of Abraham.) He called them by the names which his father had called them." Isaac digs two more wells, but the Philistines also demand those; finally, after digging a third well, the Philistines leave him alone. Isaac continues on to Beersheba; and then, after all this, Abimelech comes to offer Isaac a treaty.

Every commentary approaches this text with one question in mind: What relevance do these wells have? The purpose of the biblical record is to inspire and enlighten future generations. Who once owned which well under which name thousands of years ago seems to be an unimportant detail, a narrative without any abiding purpose.

In response to this question, the Ramban offers a mystical interpretation that rereads this text as a prophecy for the future. A similar allegorical approach is taken up by many later commentators, who offer interpretations that see the wells as symbolic of the search for spirituality and inner faith.

Other commentaries see this narrative as a reflection of contemporary struggles. Saadia Gaon, who was a fierce opponent of the Karaites (who had rejected the rabbinic tradition), saw Isaac's decision to give the wells the same names as his father as underscoring the importance of preserving the traditions and customs of previous generations.

Rabbi Samson Raphael Hirsch, who lived at a time when Jews were fighting for acceptance and equal rights, saw the Philistines' jealousy of Isaac's success as a reflection of his own time; even after reentering society, Jews would remain the subject of harassment and envy. He explains that even after receiving equal rights, the struggle would continue. Jews would need to try again and again to achieve an honored place in society; and they would need to constantly aspire to become a true light unto the nations, cherished for their teachings and values.

At its core, it seems obvious that this narrative is about Isaac's response to discrimination, but what remains unclear in the text is what his actions signify. Don Isaac Abrabanel and the Ramban have contrary views on this subject. The Ramban says that Isaac left Gerar to escape the discrimination of the people there. The wells Isaac restores are not the ones in Gerar; rather, they are a second set of wells, found elsewhere, and not a matter of dispute.

This reading tells the story of compliance; Isaac acts submissively in order to avoid conflict with the people of Gerar. (Abrabanel notes that this is why the Ramban sees no real purpose to this text. By the Ramban's reading, Isaac does nothing.) But the Ramban's reading is a forced, contorted explanation, because it assumes that the text is talking about two different sets of wells that were closed up by the Philistines—an interpretation that is divorced from the simple reading of the text.

Don Isaac Abrabanel offers a very different perspective. While Isaac does move from Gerar, he does so for a logistical reason; the land cannot accommodate his livestock and the livestock of others. But Isaac remained very close by, despite the Philistines' demands that he leave. Abrabanel then explains that "Isaac lived there against their desires, and not only that, he dug again the wells that they had closed. And to further assert his rights, he gave the wells the exact same names his father had."

Abrabanel reads this text as a story of defiance. This is even more remarkable because, until this point, Isaac has been passive, his life guided by others: he was nearly sacrificed by his father, had his wife chosen by his father's servant, and he settled in Gerar because God told him to. Isaac rises to the occasion and defies Abimelech. When the chips are down, even Isaac will stand up for his father's legacy.

Abrabanel's explanation of the wells is exactly what we need right now. Defiance isn't only found in confrontation; it is found in resilience, too. Yes, many times during Jewish history we have had to retreat; many times Jews looked like the Ramban's description of Isaac, a man who avoids conflict with a more powerful adversary. But the overarching theme of Jewish history is that Jews will find a way to make a comeback, even after failures, retreats, and catastrophes. No matter how disappointing a defeat may be, the Jews will not give up, and will return to dig the wells again and again.

A nation that knows how to rebuild what is destroyed is here to stay. And that is the magic of the twice-dug well.

This magic can be found all over Israel. Sivan Rahav Meir shared a fascinating Whatsapp message written by Nogah Ashkenazi, a German convert to Judaism. Nogah wrote that when the war started, she planned on immediately returning to her family in Germany; they were urging her to come back home. But then Nogah decided to stay. She was part of a local Whatsapp group, and there, she read her neighbors' messages to each other. Those messages are what changed her mind.

She wrote a message to her Whatsapp group to explain:

> "My first thought was to leave everything and fly to Germany to my parents with the children. My family was already preparing for our arrival.
>
> But when I opened this group on Monday and saw all the messages here, and saw all the strong women, and how you put all your efforts to help on all fronts with whatever is needed, I was so impressed. I was amazed to see the

strength of our nation. And it just kept getting even more and more impressive. This is what changed my mind.

I am not going to run away, not going to leave, because I too am very much a part of all of this. I am Jewish, and this is what I chose; and this is the vow I made in front of the Rabbis during conversion, and more importantly, the vow I made in front of God. Germany is no longer my home; I am not German, I am Jewish, and this is my place.

And I'm not leaving. On the contrary, I have become even more Jewish in my identity.

So I want to thank each of you for supporting me. My family in Germany doesn't understand my choice, and I can't blame them. You don't know what it is to be part of the Jewish people if you haven't lived it with every cell in your body...."

This is a powerful message, a declaration of the Jewish spirit. Even though Nogah is new to the Jewish people, she speaks with Isaac's voice. It is a voice of defiance, which refuses to accept destruction and persecution.

Today, as we fight another conflict near Gerar, Isaac's example will guide us. We will find strength in each other, comfort in our dreams, and hope in our history.

And no matter what, we will restore, we will rebuild, we will return.

A Letter From Israel:
It's the Time to Start Dreaming
Vayetze / November 28

It is a landscape of horror.

Kfar Aza, one of the Kibbutzim ravaged during the Hamas massacre, is filled with rubble and burned-out buildings. The terrorists came ready with gasoline and tires to burn down the homes of those who wouldn't leave their safe rooms.

While all of the bodies have already been taken for burial, there are still outlines on the grass where they had been, unmoved, for over a week. We heard firsthand reports of the horrible deaths and the extreme sadism of the terrorists. Shock, heartbreak, and anger competed for control of my heart.

I was visiting Israel as part of a group from Kehilath Jeshurun and Ramaz. But this was not a vacation excursion; instead, our group came to witness the destruction of October 7th, and the pain and suffering left in its wake.

One stop was at Shurah, the army base tasked with processing the 1,200 people murdered during this massacre. Rabbi Bentzi Mann, who was first called to serve at this base on October 8th, spoke about the overwhelming task of identifying and securing a dignified burial for the dead. He told us that in the first days, refrigerator trucks that ordinarily transport chocolate milk and yogurt were filled with bodies instead; when they would open the doors to remove the bodies, blood would come pouring out. Now, every time he sees a yogurt truck, Bentzi is reminded of death.

These difficult stories were everywhere we went; we heard from people who had witnessed the murders of their loved ones. We spoke to the families of hostages and visited the wounded in hospitals. We saw firsthand the pain and horror Israelis are experiencing.

We saw more than heartbreak. We met heroes who on October 7th, rushed to the south on their own accord to take on the attackers; we met medics who risked their lives to pull the wounded out of the battle zone.

At one point, we stopped at a gas station. Coincidentally, it turned out that the cashier Masad, from Israel's Bedouin community, was a courageous hero who had saved the lives of 14 people on October 7th. We visited grassroots organizations that are helping evacuees from the North and the South; we met with doctors who have been working 16 hours a day, and volunteers who have given up their jobs to help those in need full-time. This sense of unity is what is holding Israel together right now.

Most inspiring is that Israelis are still dreaming.

On Shabbat in Jerusalem, we read Parshat Vayetze, which begins with Jacob's dream. Aristotle called hope "a waking dream"; and in every culture dreams are a metaphor for hope.

Jacob's dream is steeped in hope. He sees a ladder on which angels go up and down; it symbolizes God sending His emissaries down to earth to watch over Jacob.

Jacob has this vision at the lowest point in his life, when he's being chased away from home and his brother Esau wants to murder him.

And now Jacob has his dream. Now Jacob finds hope. The message to the reader is that at the worst moments in life, one needs to dream the most. As Langston Hughes put it:

"Hold fast to dreams
For if dreams die
Life is a broken-winged bird
That cannot fly."

Jacob holds fast to his dream, and it changes his perspective. Rashi explains that after he woke up, Jacob's "heart lifted his feet up," because he was now filled with hope.

Jews have always understood that you are what you dream. Rabbi Levi Yitzchak of Berditchev points out in his commentary that the Hebrew word for dreaming, "chalom", is similar to the word for healing, "hachlamah". And that is because dreams of hope can give a tattered soul the strength to continue forward.

Right now in Israel, there are still dreams amidst all of the nightmares. On Shabbat morning I joined the *aufruf* of Yoni, the son of dear friends. At the Kiddush, Yoni, a soldier so devoted his commanding officer had to send him home for the *aufruf*, gave a d'var Torah. In Jacob's dream, the ladder's feet are on Earth and its head extends into heaven; Yoni explained that this is symbolic of the times we are in. Even if the ladder is stuck in our muddy and ugly reality, our heads must always be in the skies, filled with vision and values.

This vision is one and the same as Isaiah's, who tells us that, one day, swords will be beaten into plowshares. And, as Yoni reminded us, we must not forget this, even now. Yes, it is a horrible time; unquestionably there are many Palestinian civilians who are suffering profoundly in this war. Of course, it must be pointed out where the blame lies. They are largely in harm's way because Hamas has turned all of Gaza into human shields; Hamas relishes civilian casualties because they are of strategic value to this terror group. Supporters of Israel are sometimes reluctant to speak about the tragedy of Palestinian civilian casualties because it has been weaponized by Hamas and its enablers.

But that is no reason for us to forget Isaiah's dream—and there are so many who have not lost sight of this vision. Eli Beer, the CEO of United

Hatzalah, has a son who is a medic and serves in an elite combat unit. The soldiers don't have cell phones on duty, and can only speak to their families sporadically. When Eli spoke to his son, he asked him to share the highlight of the previous week; and Eli's son told him that he had found a 12-year-old Palestinian girl who was injured, who he treated and sent to Soroka Hospital in Beersheba. Isaiah's dream is still alive even during this bitter War.

There are many other inspiring dreams everywhere. I met Shelli Shemtov, whose son Omer is one of the hostages. She told me that she's keeping his room exactly as Omer left it, cluttered and messy. She said that when he gets home (and I emphasize, she said "when"), she will hug him, and then kick him in the behind and tell him to go clean up his room.

What an inspiring mother, what a powerful dream.

Racheli Fraenkel, who spent Shabbat with our group, spoke to me about the "Day of Unity" she and her husband established after the kidnapping and murder of her son Naftali in 2014. She mentioned to me that this year, and in the years to come, this day will be even more important. Israel was on the brink of civil war just days before October 7th; unity was a distant possibility. Now, after this catastrophe, we must dream once again of unity.

In Kfar Aza, we were taken around by Doron Libstein, whose late brother Ofir had been the head of the regional council. Ofir was among the first people murdered. Doron took us to the spot where Ofir was killed and asked us to sing Hatikvah, Israel's anthem of hope.

Doron has hopes and dreams. He wants to help Kfar Aza rebuild, and become bigger and better. He wants to bring more people to this beautiful corner of the Negev and fill it with life and vibrancy once again.

That is Doron's dream. And we all must dream with him—because dreams have kept the Jewish people alive.

We know that at the worst of times, we need dreams more than ever.

And now is one of those times.

Now is a time to dream.

Wrestling Lessons:
A Sermon About the KJ Mission to Israel

Vayishlach / December 4

When will the war be over? Last week in Israel, this question came up multiple times in conversation. Our group had the privilege of eating lunch last Shabbat with Benny Gantz, and we asked him the same question. At the time, there was a ceasefire; some soldiers were coming home for the weekend, and everyone seemed to catch their breath once again. But this was only a temporary lull; Hamas is still in power, and hostages are still in captivity. Unfortunately, as Gantz and many others explained, there is no quick solution; the war may take many months to achieve its objectives.

This was a difficult answer for us to hear. Everyone wants things to go back to normal as soon as possible.

We want our hostages home, we want our soldiers home, we want the evacuees back in their homes.

But sometimes there aren't any quick answers. Sometimes you must wrestle instead.

Our Torah reading includes the passage about Jacob's wrestling match with the angel. They wrestle for hours until morning; this match only ends because the angel begs Jacob to let him leave.

The Hebrew word for wrestling, "vayeavek", emphasizes how tedious and uncomfortable wrestling is. The Ramban offers two theories regarding the origin of the word. One is that it's related to the Hebrew word for hugging, "*chibuk*"; wrestlers hold each other close as they grapple in excruciating intimacy with their enemy. The other is that "*vayeavek*" is related to the Hebrew word for dust, "*avak*". Wrestling is a very slow form of combat; the feet of wrestlers are constantly shifting, in search of a more advantageous position. When wrestlers wrestle, they kick up a lot of dust.

In short, wrestling is both painful and painfully slow. But the very name Israel was born in a wrestling match. At daybreak, the angel changes Jacob's name to "Israel", in recognition of Jacob's courage; the angel declares to Jacob, "You have struggled with God and with humans and have overcome," and these words in Hebrew contain the root of the word "Israel."

Here we need to pause for a moment. Names are powerful reflections of plans and perspectives. Is the Torah suggesting that the people of Israel are fated to wrestle?

And the answer is: absolutely yes.

Wrestling is part of every life; there are no easy solutions for life's endless challenges. This is certainly true for a people who have held tight to their destiny for 3,300 years.

In order to survive, an aptitude for wrestling must be part of Jewish DNA.

Jews are once again facing a wrestling match, and the lessons of Jacob's struggle with the angel are now more important than ever. With that in mind, I'd like to share three insights from this section of the Torah.

The first is: you know it won't be easy.

Side by side with this horrific massacre in Israel is a dramatic uptick in antisemitism around the world. Many Jews have been stunned by this. In truth, I am among them. Had you asked me a few years ago, I would have told you that antisemitism was disappearing.

But now antisemitism is back with enormous intensity. This is profoundly disconcerting. But that's only *because we had the wrong expectations*. We had forgotten that being a Jew won't always be easy, that wrestling is a part of Jewish destiny.

At the same time, this attack by Hamas shocked Israel, which was completely unprepared. As Ronen Bergman reported yesterday in the New York Times, although Israeli intelligence had reliable reports of a planned Hamas attack, they dismissed them as improbable.

This type of mistake is sadly a common one. People evaluate the future based on what they see in the present; they also have a predisposition to optimism and tend to accept the most positive view of the future. The desire "to dwell in tranquility" caused Israel to forget the most important rule: it won't come easy. And frankly, you can't expect a high-tech fence to fight a war. Just ask the French; it didn't work in World War II either.

The first, and most difficult, wrestling lesson is: it doesn't come easy. Not life, not being a Jew. But this name change reminds us that we can handle it. We are Israel, we are wrestlers.

And we are fortunate to have so many heroes ready to wrestle.

Dan Polisar of Shalem College spoke to our group about his son, a commander currently on duty in Gaza. A piece of rubble had fallen on his helmet, and he was taken to the hospital to be checked out. Thankfully, he was fine, but the doctor wanted him to stay home for a few days of monitoring. But that outcome was not acceptable; the commander knew his troops needed him. So, Dan and his son argued with the doctor; she still refused to let him go. They insisted she speak to her supervisor. That didn't work, so they insisted that she speak to the head of the hospital; finally, the medical staff reluctantly allowed this devoted commander to return.

But Dan related one other point, which was the most powerful part of this story. During the back and forth with the doctor, Dan and his son were discussing their problem in the waiting room. There, a soldier, who Dan described as having "a bruise the size of Texas on his arm," saw them talking and asked them what had happened. When the soldier heard their predicament, he laughed and said: "Who cares if the doctor doesn't give you permission? Just grab a transport and go back to Gaza!"

Jacob gets injured during his wrestling match, but he forges ahead; so do these heroes, bruises and all. Yes, wrestling isn't easy. Israel's soldiers know that, but they are ready to take on the challenge anyway.

The second lesson is: help those who are wrestling.

At the end of the wrestling match, the angel injures Jacob on his thigh. Because of that, the Torah tells us that Jews are forbidden from eating the sciatic nerve.

But the reason is somewhat unclear. Why would we commemorate this injury, and why with a prohibition?

The 13th-century French Rabbi Hizkuni offers a fascinating explanation. He says that the prohibition against eating the sciatic nerve is a penalty; Jacob's family is being punished because Jacob was left alone and vulnerable. Jacob's sons should have been with him that fateful night; instead, they neglected their father and left him unaccompanied.

That was wrong. And so, for generations, Jews have accepted this penalty and not eaten the sciatic nerve.

You must not allow someone to wrestle alone.

We can be proud of how united the Jewish people are right now. In Israel, everybody is getting involved, whether it is soldiers in the reserves or volunteers in the streets.

We met an injured soldier who was fighting alongside Yossi Hershkovitz *z"l*, the principal of the Pelech High School for Boys in Jerusalem; prior to that, Yossi had taught at SAR. Hershkovitz died when a booby-trapped tunnel claimed his life.

The injured soldier told us that all of the younger members of the unit asked Hershkovitz why he reported. Hershkovitz was 44, had five children, and was exempt from service. Hershkovitz told them that he was there because the younger soldiers needed his experience and his help. He wasn't going to let them remain alone.

This is the story of Israel today: remarkable sacrifices, all in the cause of helping each other.

The Jews of America are doing their part as well. A few weeks ago, there was an unprecedented rally, where 290,000 people stood in solidarity with Israel. To my mind, the most powerful speech came from Natan Sharansky, who explained to the crowd why unity matters. He spoke about how he and his friends resisted against the former Soviet Union, and said:

> Many people thought that our cause was hopeless. How could a few men and women beat an empire all on their own?
>
> But we knew very well that we weren't truly alone. Israel and the Jewish People stood with us. From the small demonstration that four students organized at Columbia University in 1964, to the massive rally when 250,000 Jews gathered right here in this very place in 1987, three generations of World Jewry dedicated themselves to our struggle. Many of your grandparents fought for us. Many of your parents fought for us. Many of you fought for us. And this fact, this togetherness, gave me strength in my years in the Soviet Gulag.
>
> My jailors tried to tell me that I am alone, that I am doomed, that our struggle will fail. But all I had to do was to remember the many Jewish visitors who came to see us in Moscow over the years to know that they were lying. I

knew you. I knew how devoted and loving you were. I knew that we were one fighting family. And so I knew that there was only one possible outcome for our joint struggle....victory.

Coming together matters. That's why our mission went to Israel. And at every stop we were thanked for coming, by cab drivers, soldiers, and even by Benny Gantz.

And that is why I tell everyone I see that they must go visit Israel now. We cannot allow Jacob to wrestle alone.

The third lesson is: we are wrestling for something bigger.

The night after the conclusion of the mission I went to the wedding of our friends' son Yoni Troy, to Tali Miller. It was a beautiful wedding, a marriage of two children from families that had made Aliyah, who are now building their own home together in Israel.

Underneath the chuppah, there were several prayers recited. An uncle of the bride recited the prayer for the Israeli soldiers. Cousins of the groom, whose homes are on the Gaza border, recited a prayer for those who have been evacuated. And Naor, Yoni's commanding officer, who had rushed in from his base and was still in uniform, recited a prayer for the hostages. Naor is from Sderot; ten people he knew, including family members, were killed, and five others were taken hostage. There was not a dry eye when Naor recited the prayer.

Afterward, something troubled me. Here we were, at the picture-perfect Jewish wedding of two wonderful people from two wonderful families in Israel. For centuries, Jews have prayed under the chuppah "od yishamah b'arei Yehuda", that soon we would return to Israel, and the rejoicing of brides and grooms would once again be heard in the cities of Judea. And now we were at a wedding in the hills of Judea, where everything we prayed for has come true; and even so, we have to offer these heartbreaking prayers.

The question is: What point was there in praying for weddings in Israel for all these centuries, when today, weddings in Israel need new prayers?

But the answer is simple: the centuries of wrestling were for something bigger than comfort or happiness.

Yes, Israel comes with crises, challenges, and hardships.

But we're back in our homeland.

Herman Wouk, the playwright and novelist, visited Israel in 1955. He was invited by David Ben-Gurion, who was out of politics at the time, to visit him in Sde Boker in the Negev. At that point, *fedayeen* terrorists were regularly invading from Gaza, and they needed Wouk to return to Tel Aviv, with an army escort, before sunset.

At the end of the visit, Ben-Gurion turned to Wouk and said, "When are you moving to Israel? You know that this is the only place for Jews like you. You know only here you will be free."

Wouk responded with a bit of shock. He said: "Free? Free? The enemy has armies surrounding you, their leaders publicly threatening to wipe out the Zionist entity, your roads are impassable after sundown, and you say that you're free?"

Ben-Gurion responded, "I did not say safe. I said free."

And that was the ultimate lesson of our trip. We've seen Israel at a difficult time, but this is also Israel's finest hour. We are wrestling once again, and that's never easy; but we are wrestling for something bigger. And thank God we have our own sovereignty, our own state, our own army.

Thank God we're free.

And that's worth wrestling for.

Dear Anna:
A Chanukah Message
for College Students

Chanukah / December 11

Note: "Anna" in the following letter is a composite, and is based on conversations I have had with multiple students and their parents, as well as some media reports.

Dear Anna:

I am just as furious as you with Liz Magill's demeanor during her testimony before Congress. The university presidents of Penn, Harvard, and MIT all mumbled and stumbled when asked how they would classify calls for "the genocide of Jews." (They invoked the importance of free speech, an argument that, knowing how quickly anything politically incorrect is canceled at these universities, was transparently hypocritical.) But it was the complete lack of emotion that made me angriest. These three presidents all know how vulnerable Jewish students like you feel; yet, when asked about calls to kill Jews, not one of them could show the slightest bit of emotion. Instead, we got pablum and legalese, topped off with a condescending smirk from Magill.

Anna, your generation was supposed to reap the benefits of 78 years of achievement. After the Holocaust, Jews created a comfortable home for themselves in the United States and built a flourishing homeland in Israel. Your parents and grandparents worked overtime so that you could have a better life than any previous generation of Jews. On October 6th, everything was going according to plan. And then Hamas attacked.

Anna, you told me with tears in your eyes how shocked you were by the depravity of Hamas. They burned people alive, beheaded babies, and committed brutal sexual violence against women. For a few days, it even looked like Israel's very existence hung in the balance. The sheer evil of it was bewildering—not just to you, but to all of us. After watching the gruesome videos of this attack, one had to wonder: where is God? Even rabbis have been grappling with their own beliefs. Israeli TV did a feature on the Shura Army Base, where the 1,200 people murdered by Hamas were processed for burial. The rabbis and soldiers there had the agonizing task of identifying the mutilated bodies. In a television report on Shura, a soldier related that in the days after October 7th, a senior rabbi at Shura stopped participating in the daily services. When asked why, he explained: "I'm not ready to speak to God just yet."

Hamas's attack has inspired admirers around the world to attack Jews as well. There has been an explosion in antisemitism in the United States. And Anna, students like you have borne the brunt of this attack. Antisemitism has exploded on campus; 73% of Jewish students have reported experiencing or witnessing incidents, and 37% feel compelled to hide their Jewish identity. Hillels have been invaded, and Jewish students have been assaulted, spit at, and cursed at; death threats have been posted publicly on campus discussion boards.

Those who don't attack Jews are often indifferent. It is now fashionable to ignore Jewish concerns; that's exactly what you saw when the university presidents testified before Congress. One student mentioned to me that she doesn't know who she can invite to her birthday party; friends who supported the same progressive causes as she does have been steadfastly supporting Hamas. How can you socialize with someone who says that the victims at the Nova festival deserved to be killed? Signs of kidnapped Israelis are torn down by fellow students, or even worse, defaced with the word "occupier." The propaganda of Hamas is ubiquitous, with many students accepting conspiracy theories that Israel staged the massacre. The chant of "from the river to the sea," has been mainstreamed, even though it clearly suggests that the historic Jewish homeland must now be *Judenrein*, one way or another.

On campus, "Zionist" is used as a pejorative, and Israelis are slandered and called Nazis. I know your heart aches for civilian deaths in Gaza. That is the Jewish way, one that goes back to the book of

Genesis. When Jacob expected war with Esau, he prayed that he would avoid killing any of the innocent in battle. We continue to pray fervently for that today. But at the same time, Anna, you know exactly who is responsible for the deaths of Palestinians: Hamas. Michael Walzer, the foremost contemporary expert on just war theory, wrote last week: "Hamas benefits from civilian deaths; it isn't indifferent to the fate of the people it rules, it has a positive interest in their suffering."

Hamas uses human shields and calculates the strategic value of civilian deaths; it considers the death of Palestinians as beneficial to its "100-year war." Hamas trades in human suffering, filming and publicizing their own massacre to cause maximum anguish, taking hostages and then dangling them in front of their families. They are an army of sadists, driven by hatred. And they have murdered, tortured, and raped your fellow Jews, just because they are Jews. Anna, you have tried to talk to your friends about this, but they just turn away. You feel betrayed.

This betrayal extends to your professors, who have used regularly scheduled classes to "explain" the conflict in Gaza. During these lectures, Jewish students are bullied into silence. And when students like you turn to the administration, what can they expect? On Tuesday, all of America saw that from the president on down, these universities have been complicit in making Jewish students feel unwanted.

Anna, I know you feel alone. But sometimes being a Jew is going to be lonely. Generation after generation of Jews have learned how to go against the stream, to stand proud despite the jeers of haters and bullies. In many ways, that is the very lesson of Chanukah.

Chanukah is about the power of the few. A handful of Maccabees took on the Seleucid empire in a war of the few against the many. The ritual of the Menorah reinforces this theme. After the war, only one jar of oil is found, but that one jar is more than enough. One small candle is lit on the darkest, coldest night of the year, and yet it brings light to every Jew. And that is the point. Anna, you don't need to be a part of the biggest and noisiest group. You just have to bring the light.

Anna, the lesson of Chanukah is critical to students like you. On campuses, they hound you and gaslight you. They demand that you renounce your birthright and surrender to the majority. These tactics are not new at all. Medieval Christian polemicists offered the same arguments. First the gaslighting: Jews were condemned for killing Jesus in the past, even though Crusaders were murdering Jews right then and there in the present. These polemicists argued that the Jews were a dying, disappearing people who had been rejected by God; it was time for Jews to join Christianity, the winning team. Today, new polemicists demand that Jewish students bow to the majority and accept the wisdom of a noisy rabble.

Anna, Chanukah reminds us of the power that a small, dedicated group of people has. That was true 2,200 years ago, and that is true now. You and your friends have proven yourself equal to the challenge. You have come together as a community and stood up as activists. There are overflowing crowds at Hillel events. As Molly Goldstein said in an interview: "We've had Shabbat dinners filling the capacity of the kosher dining hall." In the face of all the threats and hatred, Jewish students have rededicated themselves to the Jewish people. This rededication is what Chanukah is all about.

While the holiday of Hanukkah started in Israel, it became far more significant in exile. Wherever they were, a handful of candles reminded Jews that they didn't need to give up. Even the few can triumph if they maintain their resolve.

Anna, you and your friends have been resolute. Bella Ingber, an NYU student who spoke to congressional leaders this week, concluded her speech by saying: "I am a proud Jew, and I am a proud Zionist. I am the granddaughter of Holocaust survivors. We are not going anywhere."

Anna, students like you and Bella have added another page to the Hanukkah story; you have told the world that the Jews are here to stay and not going anywhere. And I am so proud of what you have accomplished. I know that if you are our future leaders, the Jewish future is very bright.

Chag Sameach!

The Optimism of Seven Lean Years
Miketz / December 15

Optimism is human nature. The neuroscientist Tali Sharot, in her book *The Optimism Bias*, shows that optimism cuts across all cultures. She draws the conclusion that humans are hotwired to imagine an unrealistic picture of the future. It is instinctive to dream of "happy ever after," even if that often is not the case.

The belief in progress is equally instinctive, because it is nurtured by optimism—and it is just as irrational. In 1992, Francis Fukuyama, a political scientist, wrote *The End of History*. He saw the fall of the Soviet Union as the ultimate triumph of the Western democratic order and the culmination of all history. There would be no further conflicts, now that the world had seen the light.

Unfortunately, that was not true. New dictators arose, and democracy has been on the decline since he wrote the book.

But the failure of optimism doesn't mean we should reject it. Redemption is one of the foundational beliefs of Judaism. Jeremiah held out hope that a newly exiled nation would return home; Isaiah imagined a world filled with peace and harmony. Jews are called by Zechariah "prisoners of hope"; our souls' first language is optimism.

Since October 7th, Jews have felt betrayed by optimism. History has gone backward. It feels like it's 1948 again, with Israel fighting for its very existence. Every dream seems counterfeit. Optimism feels like a cognitive trap that offers false hope when hope is pointless.

It is here where optimism needs an unlikely ally to succeed: pessimism. That is a central lesson of Joseph's dreams.

Joseph's life story revolves around three sets of dreams. The first two he has as a child, when he is the spoiled younger half-brother who is deeply resented by his siblings. He dreams that they are in the field, and his bundle of grain rises up, and the bundles of his brothers are bowing to him. Then Joseph has another dream, where the sun and the moon and the stars are all bowing to him.

These dreams seemingly need no interpretation. Joseph is declaring himself the ruler of his brothers.

Immediately, the opposite happens. The dreams stir the brothers' jealousy, and they sell him into slavery in Egypt.

The second set of dreams occur when Joseph is in an Egyptian prison, and two fellow prisoners, the butler and the baker, ask him to interpret their dreams; Joseph does so accurately, predicting that the butler will be freed and the baker will be executed. Two years later, the butler will recommend Joseph as a dream interpreter.

The third set are Pharaoh's dreams. He has two dreams. In one, seven fat cows are swallowed up by seven skinny cows; in the second, seven healthy stalks of grain are devoured by seven sickly stalks of grain.

Joseph is called from prison to interpret Pharaoh's dreams; he explains that there will be seven years of plenty, followed by seven years of famine. Luckily, Joseph explains, the dreams offer a timely warning, which will allow Egypt to get ready for the famine and overcome it. Joseph so impresses Pharaoh that he is immediately named the viceroy of Egypt.

What jumps out at the reader is the way Pharaoh's dreams stand in sharp contrast with Joseph's dreams.

Pharaoh's dreams project a tragic ending; but because Pharaoh shared them, they will have a positive ending. Joseph's dreams project a very happy ending for him; but because Joseph shared them, he ends up a slave.

Pharaoh's dreams are difficult to interpret; he turns to all of his priests for answers, but they have none. It is clear that God is communicating with Pharaoh. In contrast, Joseph's dreams are obvious and need no interpretation. His brothers assume that these dreams are the product of Joseph's imagination and nothing more.

The most fascinating contrast has to do with what occurs after a double dream. Pharaoh's double dream indicates that it will come true immediately; Joseph's double dream seems to wait for a long time to come true.

There are many lessons that these contrasts teach. First of all, be wary of happy endings. Joseph's dreams feed his own vanity, and make him oblivious to his own brother's hatred; in fact, his dreams make their hatred worse. This is a good dream that causes damage, a sunny picture of the future that is actually a liability.

Second, one must recognize that pessimism often allows optimism to succeed. Pharaoh's nightmares allow for proper preparation, to be ready for the upcoming famine. The unhappy ending in the dream actually helps Pharaoh achieve a happy ending in real life. This is a bad dream that does a great deal of good, preparing Egypt for the future.

Third, good dreams often have a very long runway. Joseph explains to Pharaoh that the double dream means "that the matter has been determined by God, and that God will soon carry it out." This is a bold assertion, considering that Joseph's own double dream had not yet come true.

However, I would argue that that isn't the case; Joseph's dreams actually came true immediately. What his brothers thought to be a mere figment of Joseph's ambition was actually a divine prophecy.

However, both the brothers and Joseph misunderstood this dream; they assumed it meant that Joseph would be the recipient of great privilege, an entitled ruler who receives unearned gifts. But actually, the purpose of the dream was to call Joseph to be a true leader, to be a servant of both his family and all of Egypt.

In order to do that, Joseph would have to learn humility. In order to become an authentic leader, Joseph would need to overcome great challenges. And so he is sold into slavery immediately, which prepares him for the fulfillment of his dream.

Joseph could only achieve this dream through great difficulty. But the pain and suffering he endured as a slave got him ready for his ultimate role. And in the happiest of endings for the entire family, Joseph was in the exact right place to save them from the famine.

Right now it is difficult to dream, and optimism is scarce. But the lesson of our Torah reading is that there are no grand dreams of the future without difficulty and sacrifice. Pessimism plays a supporting role right alongside optimism. If we learn how to prepare for the famine, we will be able to endure until there is a happy ending.

And we have known this all along. In 1956, Moshe Dayan gave a eulogy for Roi Rotberg, a 21-year-old soldier who was ambushed in the fields of Nahal Oz, near Gaza. This eulogy is prescient; it speaks directly to us today in the aftermath of October 7th. Dayan explained that Israel must never be lulled into complacency, imagining that everything will be okay. A country like Israel has enemies and must be ready. He said: "That is our generation's fate and our life's choice -- to be willing and armed, strong and unyielding, lest the sword be knocked from our fist and our lives cut down."

It was difficult to contemplate this reality in 1956 when burying Roi Rotberg, a young soldier who was brutally killed on a Kibbutz. It is even more difficult to contemplate this reality in 2023. Dayan's eulogy is painfully pessimistic.

But like Pharaoh's nightmarish dream, this bitter pessimism is the only way forward to a better future. Ordinary optimism might cause us to overestimate what can be, and imagine that we can simply be carefree. But optimism is not a blank check.

Mature optimism is something different; it walks hand in hand with pessimism, to enable one to be ready for each day's crisis. Tomorrow will be another day, another opportunity for hope. But not today. We must not lose sight of reality.

What gives me optimism now is how Israelis are heroically carrying the burden of an awful time; they stand ready to meet the challenges of the seven lean years. Shai Bernstein (whose father, Dr. David

Bernstein, taught at Ramaz for many years) wrote a powerful note about his service in Gaza:

"I've seen with my own eyes.

I've seen injured friends in the hospital who, despite the pain and long recovery process that await them, seem way stronger than me.

I've seen Colonel Asaf Chamami's mom at his Shiva; I almost fell apart right in front of her eyes. She was the strong one, not me.

I've seen teachers, doctors, factory workers, and people working in tech, leaving their jobs and families, leaving everything they have and fighting like lions.

I've seen Matan (who voted for Meretz), Jonathan (Lapid), Guy (Bibi), and Itamar (Gantz) having a fierce political argument.

It looked like a competition of who loved the State of Israel more.

I've seen the same four chevra leap with all of their gear into the breach, together as one.

I've seen them run to aid the injured after the missile hit us, even though the bullets were still flying over their heads. Each one carrying the stretcher, lending a shoulder, together.

I've seen communities across the US buckling down, raising money and working hard to send supplies, to support the soldiers and citizens of Israel. (Some of the letters we got from kids were so simple, yet special and moving — you could cry).

I've seen a polarized and divided nation that became united in an instant.

We realize that we're fighting not only for our lives, but for our very right to exist."

This letter chronicles the pain of young men and women leaving their families, of injured soldiers in the hospital, of parents burying their children. And yet the letter is not at all pessimistic. It is inspiring that people like Shai are willing to carry the burden of the seven lean years and ensure a better future.

And even during a nightmare, that is worthy of optimism.

We Must Never Forget Them

Vaera / January 12

One could call this the Gettysburg Address of the Exodus. At the beginning of Parshat Vaera, God speaks to Moses and assures him that slavery is about to come to an end:

> Therefore say to the children of Israel: "I am the Lord; I will bring you out from under the burdens of the Egyptians, I will rescue you from their bondage, and I will redeem you with an outstretched arm and with great judgments. I will take you as My people, and I will be your God. Then you shall know that I am the Lord your God who brings you out from under the burdens of the Egyptians. And I will bring you into the land which I swore to give to Abraham, Isaac, and Jacob; and I will give it to you as an inheritance."

In just a few sentences, the Torah previews the full process of redemption; not just an escape from slavery, but the creation of a new nation with a homeland of their own. The Talmud refers to the first four verbs in this section (bring out, rescue, redeem, and take) as the "four languages of redemption". To this day, the four cups of wine at Passover Seder are in celebration of these words.

The parsha begins with this speech, most probably in order to begin on a high point. But it also begins mid-conversation, which strips it of context. God's words are actually a response to an angry challenge by Moses; after his initial petition to Pharaoh backfires, and causes even greater pain to the slaves, Moses turns to God and says: "Lord, why have you done such evil to this nation? Why is it that You have sent me?"

Moses's words border on the sacrilegious. Indeed, several commentaries criticize Moses for this. Rashi says that God, in his response, subtly rebukes Moses for his complaint; one Midrash says Moses was later punished for challenging God, and not allowed to enter Israel.

Yet the simple reading of God's response is that He takes Moses's challenge seriously; that is why God offers such a thorough and detailed reply. Moses is speaking on behalf of those who are oppressed and downtrodden, and even if he speaks with chutzpah, he does so out of love for his Jewish brothers and sisters.

Another Midrash amplifies Moses's complaint. Moses knows the Jews will eventually be rescued, but he cannot tolerate the delay. A future redemption, Moses says, will not "help the Jews who are now being thrown under the building." This curious phrase refers to a shocking image found in

Rabbinic literature that in the Egyptian construction projects of Pithom and Raamses, Jews were used as bricks, and squeezed into the gaps of walls. A similar Midrash asserts that Pharaoh sought to heal himself of leprosy by bathing in the blood of 150 murdered Jewish children each morning and evening.

These midrashim images amplify the biblical text, which recounts Pharaoh's attempts to murder Jewish children. But the midrashim are not here just to vilify Pharaoh; they come to expose the inner workings of his regime.

Some acts of hatred are utilitarian; one feels threatened, and therefore needs to fight an enemy. But other times, hatred stands at the very foundation of a society. The historian Saul Friedlander coined the term "redemptive antisemitism" to describe the Nazi hatred of Jews. The Nazis saw Jews as a virus that weakens humanity; therefore, the destruction of the Jews would bring goodness to the rest of the world.

These midrashim are articulating something similar. In one, the murder of Jewish children is seen as therapeutic, a way for Pharaoh to recover his health. In the other, dead Jews are the foundation of Egyptian development. For Pharaoh, killing is no longer the means of maintaining power, but the very purpose of power itself. Violence against Jews is the scaffolding that holds his regime together.

Unfortunately, these Midrashim are prescient, offering a clear description of Hamas. There are no limits to Hamas's "100-year war." It engaged in a premeditated mass murder in the most horrible, depraved fashion, all proudly recorded by terrorists on body cameras. Even more shocking is Hamas's overt contempt for the very people they claim to represent. Palestinians were Hamas's first victims, as this autocratic regime has regularly murdered its opponents. Today, Palestinians are enduring great suffering because Hamas cynically uses civilians as human shields, and calculates the strategic value of their deaths. Hamas will have the Palestinians fight to the death in Gaza while many of its leaders sit comfortably in Doha.

Supporters of Israel are sometimes reluctant to speak about the tragedy of Palestinian civilians because their deaths have been weaponized by Hamas and its enablers; as I write these words, the International Court of Justice is presiding over a South African claim that Israel has engaged in "genocide." But even so, we must mourn for the deaths of those caught in the crossfire. Every human being is created in the image of God.

Hamas has built its regime with the blood of both Palestinians and Israelis. Its great construction project, the Gaza tunnels, is built for death, and by death. Hamas's wanton violence may shock us, but the Midrash predicted this type of hatred hundreds of years ago.

Like Moses, we are anguished over the innocent babies who were massacred and mourn for those who were brutally murdered. Israel has had to send its best and brightest out to take up the fight; too many of them have fallen in battle. For all of these tragedies, we cry.

Every death is a profound loss, but the death of a young person is all the more painful because it is so unexpected. In the ordinary way of the world, children bury their parents, not the other way around. My father died in a car accident, predeceasing my grandfather by nearly 40 years. My grandfather was a jovial man, who always had a smile on his face; that is, except when he spoke about my father. Then the smile left his face; even decades later, the grief would quickly return. No suffering is greater than that of losing a child.

A Hebrew expression, which is first found in Isaiah (38:10), best describes a young death: "*nektaph b'mei chayav,*" "cut off in the middle of their days." It emphasizes that a young death is actually a double tragedy: one loses not just the person, but also what the person could have been.

Each of these deaths is painful for our entire community. News reports out of Israel recount the entire biography of those who have died; the entire Jewish world repeats their names and their stories. And inevitably, we find that we are one or two degrees of separation from these tragedies.

Hamas considers this to be Israel's strategic flaw. Yahya Sinwar sees the Israeli concern for each hostage and each soldier to be a weakness; he considers his ability to write off the lives of thousands of Palestinians to be a strength. He ridicules Israel's willingness to call a ceasefire in order to release a handful of hostages. Like Pharaoh, Sinwar is ready to build pyramids with the bodies of babies.

Sinwar is correct that brutality holds strategic value; ignoring the suffering of one's own people means that one can fight on without any limitations. But it is morally untenable. Moses cried for the babies Pharaoh was murdering, and we must follow his example.

Even if it seems foolish, we must advocate for each hostage, and cry for every soldier.

We must never forget them. And we must challenge God to remember them and put an end to their suffering now.

When Life Gives You Bitter Herbs

Bo / January 19

Bitter herbs are a culinary misfit. One can fulfill the obligation to eat the bitter herbs (Maror) at the Seder with many different sour and spicy vegetables, including Horseradish, Romaine Lettuce, and Chicory. But what is very strange about Maror is that we eat these vegetables on their own at the Seder; as the Mah Nishtanah exclaims, on any other night, no one would eat a bitter spoonful of horseradish straight up.

Maror was misunderstood from the very beginning. There is no clear indication in the Biblical text as to why it is included in the Seder. The Torah in Parshat Bo says the Passover sacrifice should be eaten "roasted in fire, with unleavened bread, and with bitter herbs...." While the Passover Sacrifice has a direct connection to the night of the Exodus, and Matzah is connected to the haste in which the Jews left Egypt, the reader is left to imagine what purpose Maror might have.

Several commentaries see Maror as a way to enhance the meat of the Passover sacrifice. The Ohr HaChaim says that "it is the way of those who eat roasted meat to do so with something sharp, for this makes it tastier, and entices people to eat more." Ibn Ezra and Ibn Kaspi offer similar interpretations. This perspective is found in the Talmud as well. It asserts that certain offerings of meat must be eaten in "the manner of royalty" and explains that the manner of royalty is to eat meat "roasted and served with mustard."

This interpretation is closest to the simple reading of the text. The Torah wants the Passover sacrifice to represent the joy of freedom, and be eaten in a royal fashion; to do so requires that it be served with an appropriate condiment.

But the Mishnah and Passover Haggadah offer a very different perspective on Maror; Rabban Gamliel says: "The reason for bitter herbs is because the Egyptians embittered our forefathers' lives in Egypt..." Maror is interpreted as a symbol of slavery, not royalty.

David Henshke argues that Rabban Gamliel's explanation reflects a shift that took place after the destruction of the Temple. There was no longer a Passover sacrifice; one needed a new rationale to include the bitter herbs at the Seder. Rabban Gamliel found a different symbolism in the Maror, one that related to the actual suffering during slavery.

But this new understanding of Maror seems strange. An evening of redemption should be filled with joy and sweetness. The point of Passover is to escape the horrors of slavery; to place bitterness at the center of the Seder plate seems to undermine Passover's message.

Most often, answers given to this question embrace the positive side of bitterness; or to put it a bit more cynically, that "suffering is good for us." Maror is a reminder that slavery has shaped the Jewish soul just as much as freedom.

Undoubtedly, suffering can improve us as people. Professors Richard Tedeschi and Lawrence Calhoun coined the term "post-traumatic growth" after observing that many of their trauma patients had reinvented themselves in the aftermath of a major tragedy. They had grown in terms of their strength of character, relationships with others, perspective on life, appreciation for life, and spirituality. Their suffering had changed them for the better.

Even before post-traumatic growth was discovered by psychologists, it was evident to philosophers and theologians. Nietzsche wrote that "to those human beings who are of any concern to me I wish suffering, desolation, sickness, ill-treatment, indignities..." because Nietzsche recognized that character is forged in the crucible of adversity. Rabbi Samson Raphael Hirsch notes that the Hebrew word for a "test of suffering" or "nisayon" is the same as the Hebrew word for "raising up" — "nissa" — because a test raises a person's character. The bitterness of suffering is itself the silver lining that carries other blessings.

The Sefat Emet makes a direct connection between this idea and Maror. He says that "the bitterness of slavery was a preparation for redemption, and this (bitterness) remains with us during the times of redemption." Maror reminds us that bitterness begets character, and is itself a gateway to redemption.

As I get older, I get increasingly uncomfortable with these types of explanations. I don't contest their truth. Yes, suffering can spur spiritual growth. And one who suffers will find the pursuit of meaning to be the best way to live with suffering; as Rabbi Joseph B. Soloveitchik wrote, "Judaism teaches us that the sufferer commits a grave sin if he allows his troubles to go to waste and remain without meaning or purpose." Spiritual quests are how the soul copes with tragedy.

But what I find deeply disturbing are articles and sermons that use this difficult truth to romanticize suffering. They depict the personal growth achieved in the face of suffering as some sort of Hollywood ending that makes it all worthwhile. But it doesn't.

The Talmud discusses an idea called "afflictions of love," which claims that the righteous suffer unnecessarily in order to receive a greater reward in the future. After a discussion of the great reward involved, it tells real-life stories about suffering. In one, Rabbi Yochanan suffers from an illness. His colleague Rabbi Chanina visits and asks: "Is your suffering dear to you?" Perhaps Rabbi Yochanan appreciated the spiritual glory of suffering and wanted to continue with his afflictions. Rabbi Yochanan offered a terse response: "Neither the sufferings nor their reward".

After a lengthy discussion of theory, the Talmud shares the real-life verdict on suffering: all the growth in the world is not worth the suffering. Maror is always bitter, and may it stay far far away from us, always.

So how else can one see Maror? The past few months have given me a new reflection on the passage of Rabban Gamliel. I now believe that Maror reminds us that even when we can proudly sing "this year in Jerusalem," there will still be Maror on the Seder plate. Despite returning to our homeland and building a remarkable state, we cannot banish the bitter herbs. Life will always have a side portion of Maror.

But the Maror at the Seder is not there to sober us up and offer us cynical realism. Instead, it reminds us that Maror is never the final chapter. Bitter herbs may be ever-present, but so is redemption. We simply have to get through this portion of Maror and start over again. We have overcome, we can overcome, and we will overcome.

In the worst of times, Jews never gave up on redemption; and now that we have experienced a taste of redemption, we certainly cannot give up on redemption, no matter how bitter things are.

This message was powerfully articulated in a heroic eulogy that a bereaved mother, Sarit Zussman, gave for her son Ben, a fallen soldier. After speaking about her remarkable son and the profound love he shared with his family, she ended by speaking to the people of Israel:

> And now to you, to all of you, to all of us, to the Jewish people in the Land of Israel. As a storyteller, I tell you: that our story has a happy ending. We are going to win. We have no other choice. We are a people who want to live, unlike our enemies, lowly and miserable, cowards, Nazis and their accomplices, who sanctify death. We will live, and thrive, and build.....Do you hear, people of Israel? World, do you hear? Do you hear, lowly enemies who desire death and evil? Am Yisrael chai – the Jewish people live, forever and ever and for all eternity, standing tall and with our heads held high...

These moving words remind us that the true lesson of Maror is that we must hold on to hope, even when it seems impossible. The Seder ends with joy, despite the Maror. No matter how difficult it gets, we must hold our heads high and proudly declare: Am Yisrael Chai!

The People's Flag
Beshalach / January 26

A country must have a flag. In 1896, Theodore Herzl wrote, "we have no flag, and we need one." Herzl offered a rather pedestrian suggestion of "a white flag, with seven golden stars. The white field symbolizes our pure new life; the stars are the seven golden hours of our working day." (However, Herzl carefully arranged the stars so that together, the seventh star is a Magen David made of the other stars.)

Flags have always played a role in statecraft. In the book of Numbers, flags organize the Jews as they travel through the desert; in later Jewish history, impromptu flags, often used on Simchat Torah, were symbols of Jewish solidarity. In the ancient world, flags, ensigns, and banners played a critical role in warfare, where they took on extraordinary importance; capturing the enemy's flag was an act of heroic valor and a humiliation for the opponent. The Romans treated their ensigns as an object of worship; Josephus writes that the Romans considered it "a terrible thing... and a great shame, if they were stolen away." In modern times, flags are primarily a national symbol.

To Herzl, having a national flag was critical. He wrote, "If we desire to lead many men, we must raise a symbol above their heads." To him, the flag was another way of transforming the humble Jewish masses into a nation. He would later write in his diary that he hoped to be remembered by history as "an impecunious Jewish journalist, [who] amid the deepest degradation of the Jewish people and at a time of the most disgusting anti-Semitism, made a flag out of a rag and a people out of a decadent rabble, and was able to rally this people around such a flag." The leader, and their flag, are what make the people a people.

Herzl, along with his flag, led the huddled masses to their promised land. However, what would ultimately become the flag of Israel represents a very different vision.

Four biblical commentators from medieval France mention flags in their commentaries on Parshat Beshalach, during a battle scene at the end of the Parsha. The newly freed slaves are ruthlessly attacked in the desert by Amalek, who "surprised [the Jews] on the march, when [they] were famished and weary, and cut down all the stragglers in [their] rear." The Jews have to fight back.

What ensues during this is quite unusual. Joshua is sent to lead the Jews in battle; at the same time, the Torah tells us:

> And Moses said to Joshua...Tomorrow I will stand on the top of the hill with the rod of God in my hand.... Moses, Aaron, and Hur went to the top of the hill. As

long as Moses held up his hands, the Israelites were winning, but whenever he lowered his hands, the Amalekites were winning. When Moses's hands grew tired, they took a stone and put it under him and he sat on it. Aaron and Hur held his hands up—one on one side, one on the other—so that his hands remained steady till sunset.

With Moses's hands held high, Joshua wins the war.

Every commentary grapples with the same question: what is Moses doing with his hands? The most obvious answer, offered by Rabbi Abraham Ben HaRambam and Shadal, is that Moses raises his hands in prayer and miraculously protects the Jewish soldiers.

Others find this explanation unsatisfying; if this was meant to be a time of miracles, why did Moses send the soldiers to begin with?

Four commentaries from Northern France — Bechor Shor, Rashbam, Chizkuni, and Yosef Karo — offer a very different interpretation. Moses held his staff high in his hands, and it functioned as a military flag. (It is fascinating that the commentaries offer three different vernacular words for flags: *banniere, confanon,* and *pendon.*) Holding the flag high strengthened the morale of the troops; Moses's staff and his hands functioned like a flag.

These two explanations are polar opposites. One sees Moses's hand-raising as the prerequisite for a miraculous intervention; the other sees Moses's staff as playing a mundane role, a rudimentary flag that rallies the troops on the ground.

The Mishnah offers a middle ground; the hands of Moses functioned as a spiritual flag. It says that when Moses held his hands aloft, "the Jewish people turned their eyes upward and subjected their hearts to their Father in Heaven; then they prevailed. But if not, they fell in battle."

For the Mishnah, the result of the war is miraculous, but the miracle doesn't belong to Moses; it belongs to the people. Moses' hands held aloft, metaphorically the first flag of the Jewish people, is not about the leader; it is about the people. It reminds the soldiers to focus on their divine connection and reflect on their mission.

The Mishnah offers a very different vision of what a flag is: it represents the shared values of the community. Its worth comes from what people project onto it and how people connect to it. Unlike Herzl, the Mishnah sees the value of the flag as dependent on what people invest in it.

Herzl's vision for a flag was rejected. Instead, a proposal by David Wolffsohn, a close associate of

Herzl and his successor as President of the Zionist Organization, was accepted. Wolffsohn writes that, at the first Zionist conference, the following inspiration came to him:

> At the behest of our leader Herzl, I came to Basel to make preparations for the Zionist Congress. Among many other problems that occupied me then was one that contained something of the essence of the Jewish problem. What flag would we hang in the Congress Hall? Then an idea struck me. We have a flag — and it is blue and white. The talith (prayer shawl) with which we wrap ourselves when we pray: that is our symbol. Let us take this Talith from its bag and unroll it before the eyes of Israel and the eyes of all nations. So I ordered a blue and white flag with the Shield of David painted upon it. That is how the national flag, that flew over Congress Hall, came into being.

Wolffsohn created a flag that reflects every man; and it also reflects the everyman, the Tallit worn on the backs of tailors and wagon drivers, the ordinary folk who understood Zionism well before the rest of the world did. It is not a top-down flag, one brought by the leader to transform a hopeless rabble; instead, it is a people's flag, one that draws its meaning from the hopes and dreams of its followers.

Rabbi Joseph B. Soloveitchik argues that the people's attachment to the Israeli flag transforms it into a sacred object. In a Yiddish lecture given at a Mizrachi convention in the 1960s, Rabbi Soloveitchik remarked that he generally doesn't understand the magical attraction of flags or other objects like it. However, the Israeli flag is different. The Shulchan Aruch says that a Jew who is murdered must be buried in the clothes he was wearing when he was killed. Soloveitchik says this law teaches us that clothing "acquires a certain sanctity when spattered with the blood of a martyr. How much more is this so of the blue and white flag, which has been immersed in the blood of thousands of young Jews who fell in battle defending the country and its population. The Israeli flag has a spark of sanctity that flows from devotion and self-sacrifice."

The people's flag carries more than the hearts and souls of a nation; it represents the sacrifices that so many people have made to build the State of Israel.

Today, our young men and women have to go into battle; far too many will not come home again. It is grueling to continue to fight against a fanatical, bloodthirsty foe. The ongoing losses are too large to bear. As the war continues, we too, like Moses, find that our hands grow weary.

What continues to hold the flag high are the people, who are filled with dedication. In the end, Moses can no longer hold up the flag; his hands need to be held aloft by Aaron and Hur. This moment offers a critical lesson: flags don't belong to leaders, not even Moses. They belong to the entire people.

Today in Israel, it is the ordinary Israeli, and only the ordinary Israeli, who has held the country together. Previously unknown heroes have rushed to the front lines, organized volunteers, and taken care of a country in crisis. These ordinary people have consecrated the flag with the sacrifices they have made, sacrifices too great to count.

Israel's flag is their flag. And they are holding it up high, despite everything.

The Ground Still Trembles

Yitro / February 2

No moment in the Bible is more magnificent, no event more central. At the revelation on Mount Sinai, the veil between the mundane and the divine was pulled away, and all assembled could see God directly.

The encounter at Mount Sinai carries great theological significance. Nachmanides says there is a daily commandment to never forget the encounter at Mount Sinai; Yehuda Halevi explains that this nationwide revelation is the foundation of the Torah. All of Judaism is a footnote to that day, an ongoing exploration of this intense spiritual singularity.

Words fail to describe that day. The Torah, in Parshat Yitro, describes something akin to a simultaneous hurricane and volcanic eruption, in which "...there were thunderings and lightning, and a thick cloud on the mountain; and the sound of the Shofar was very loud, so that all the people who were in the camp trembled...Mount Sinai was completely in smoke...Its smoke ascended like the smoke of a furnace, and the whole mountain quaked greatly."

Midrashim further dramatize this depiction. Rabbi Akiva says that the Jews saw the voice that spoke on Mount Sinai, something that is otherwise physically impossible. Other Midrashim say that all those who were blind and deaf were healed that day, and able to take part in the revelation. Another

Midrash says that the call of Sinai was heard throughout the world, and all of humanity, in a sense, stood at the foot of Mount Sinai.

Taken together, these texts emphasize that the encounter at Mount Sinai was unparalleled and transcendent, an event that will never be repeated or equaled.

So where does that leave those of us who were born too late to stand at Mount Sinai? Today, those with deeply religious souls search for God and long to hear His voice. They wait patiently for a divine calling. But sadly, there are no new Mount Sinais available, no casual daily revelations.

Most people of faith find ways to accommodate this gaping lack of inspiration. Sometimes, even an occasional glimpse of transcendence can satisfy years of spiritual cravings. But at times, we need to turn in a different direction to discover the divine.

Rav Simcha Bunim of Przysucha can help direct us. Rav Simcha Bunim was the "Un-Rebbe," a radical Chasidic leader who diminished the importance of his own position and urged his followers to find their own path. He would illustrate his view of the Rebbe's role with the following parable:

> Isaac from Krakow was a poor tailor, who was plagued by a recurring dream. In the dream, he had a vision of a large

bounty of gold which was hidden under a bridge outside the imperial palace in Prague. Night after night, this dream would repeat itself, until finally, Isaac decided he had to make the ten-day journey to Prague to find this treasure. He explained to his wife why he had to go, and started his journey.

In Prague, Isaac arrived and found the bridge just as it appeared in his dream. But he couldn't dig for the treasure, because it was always under heavy guard; the bridge was right outside the palace, after all. For three nights, Isaac studied the guards' rotations, hoping to find a pause long enough to allow him to start his search. On the third night, one of the guards grabbed him and arrested him. The guard shouted at Isaac, "You spy, I recognize you! You've been here three nights in a row, plotting against the king". Isaac, in shock, began to sputter how he was an innocent man who was there because he had had a dream about some gold hidden under the bridge. Recognizing the simple sincerity of Isaac's words, the guard released

Isaac, and with a laugh, said: "You fool, you stood there for three nights straight just because of a dream! Last night I had a dream that there's a treasure buried in the backyard of Isaac the tailor in Krakow. Do you think I'm going to travel all the way to Krakow just because of a silly dream?"

Isaac immediately returned home. When he entered his house, his wife asked him: "Where's the treasure?"

Isaac responded: "Give me a shovel and I'll show you."

Isaac went outside and dug up the gold. The Prague treasure had been hidden right in his backyard all along.

Rav Simcha Bunim used this tale as a parable about spirituality and wisdom. People chase spiritual gurus and great Rabbis in the hope of achieving spiritual heights. But in the end, what one is looking for is hiding in their own backyard, buried under a lot of nonsense.

For those in search of great revelations, Rav Simcha Bunim's parable reminds us that before looking elsewhere, we need to turn inward and find the treasures buried in our own hearts.

This is true of the encounter at Sinai as well. The Talmud relates that every child is instructed the entire Torah in their mother's womb, only to have an angel force the child to forget what they learned at birth. This text is a bit of a riddle; why teach the fetus Torah, if it is meant to ultimately forget it a few weeks later?

Rav Simcha Bunim's parable explains this text well. The Torah we once studied may be forgotten, but its imprint remains. What makes revelation compelling is that our hearts are already attuned to what is being said. There are debates among philosophers as to whether all of the commandments can be understood intellectually; but they are certainly understood by the soul, which immediately attaches itself to the divine. And that *a priori* appreciation of revelation, that knowledge before knowledge, is a treasure we carry in our own hearts. Even when we stand far away from Sinai, there is another source of inspiration right at our side.

Since October 7th, I have heard story after story of ordinary people who have done extraordinary things. When they tell others about what happened, they share one refrain: "I never imagined that I could have done this." Yet in a time of crisis, these heroes found remarkable inner strength. Ordinary Israelis took on the battle from day one, rushing to the front lines before being called up. A soldier sacrificed his own life by falling on a grenade to save his comrades' lives. Rescuers entered the Nova Festival under heavy fire and saved the lives of hundreds of participants. Dedicated parents, brothers, sisters, and children, have traveled everywhere demanding that the world bring their relatives home from captivity. A young mom built a large distribution center for evacuees in just a few days. Academics have become ad hoc military suppliers, providing much-needed protective gear to soldiers. Bereaved parents have spoken to group after group, offering strength and comfort to others even while their own hearts are broken. Amidst all the darkness and destruction, these accidental heroes heard a small, still voice of inspiration, and answered the call.

For years, I wondered if I could ever experience something like the encounter at Sinai; when would I feel the ground tremble with divine inspiration?

Now I have an answer. We stand at Sinai once again when we meet one of these heroes. They are spiritual treasures, right here in our own backyard. Listen to them, listen to their stories. It is amazing what they have done.

And the world trembles before their greatness.

We Stand with the IDF

Mishpatim / February 9

Next week, I will be taking a mission to Israel; it is my third trip there since October 7th. Like the previous two trips, we will be making an unusual stop: an army base.

Soldiers and tourists are a strange combination; in no other country do visits like these happen.

So why are we going to the army bases? Because the soldiers of the IDF are our heroes.

You would get a very different picture of the IDF on TikTok, on college campuses, and at the International Court of Justice. There, the State of Israel is libeled, and the IDF is the very focal point of demonization.

Israel (and the IDF) have been charged with genocide in this so-called court of justice, whose judges include representatives from China and Russia, well-known paragons of human rights. The ICJ filing notes that the following countries have made official claims that Israel is committing genocide: Bolivia, Brazil, Colombia, Cuba, Iran, Turkey, and Venezuela.

This recalls the well-known adage that you can judge a person by the character of their enemies. When such a rogue's gallery are your accusers, you know you must be doing something right.

There is much to be said in response to this accusation, but I will not rehash those arguments here. Suffice it to say that Bret Stephens got it right when he called the accusation of genocide against Israel a moral obscenity.

It is an obscenity because genocide is precisely what Israel's enemy Hamas is attempting to do.

It is an obscenity to equate the Jews, the victims of the worst genocide in human history, with the Nazis.

It is an obscenity because countries like North Korea, China, and Iran are treated as upstanding members of the international community, while a democracy is the subject of obsessive criticism.

It is an obscenity because it avoids even the smallest measure of truth. The Arab citizens of Israel live in freedom, while the Arab citizens of Gaza have lived in fear since Hamas took over in 2006. Arab Israelis have supported Israel in its war against Hamas; one early poll found 70% of Arab Israelis support the war. But neither before October 7th, nor since then, has there been much mention of the crimes Hamas perpetrated against its own citizens, including murdering opponents and stealing aid for the poor to build its war machine.

And the accusations against the IDF are a bald-faced lie. Yossi Klein Halevi wrote in 2014:

> "Israelis know that the IDF does not deliberately kill civilians. We know this because we are the IDF—because our

sons, our neighbors' sons, have been fighting in Gaza. We know that dead Palestinian civilians serve the interests only of Hamas, not Israel....We know that mistakes happen in war because, unlike many of Israel's critics in the West, Israelis know war. We know that houses in Gaza were booby-trapped, that schools and mosques concealed arms caches and entrances to tunnels and were repeatedly used as launching pads for rockets."

That was 2014. The more things change, the more they are the same.

This horrid accusation in The Hague is of great strategic value to Hamas. It is an ugly piece of propaganda masquerading as idealism and shapes the world's perspective on Israel. It stretches open the window of acceptable discourse about Israel and allows lies and libels to go mainstream.

Relative moderates unconsciously follow suit. *The New York Times* published an absurd article analyzing the social media accounts of Israeli soldiers who had posted insensitive TikTok videos from Gaza. Yes, they found 50 videos the reporters considered inappropriate. How is this a headline in a war that had disgusting and depraved crimes filmed with delight by Hamas? And you make a case based on 50 TikTok? Tens of thousands of Israeli troops have served in Gaza, the vast majority of whom have conducted themselves with honor.

The Times hasn't informed its readers when it will analyze TikTok accounts of other armies.

The IDF is held to a standard of perfection and criticized mercilessly for every misstep.

Where does this criticism come from? Undoubtedly, some are motivated by sympathy for the Palestinian civilians who are caught in this crossfire.

It goes without saying, although it still needs to be said, that we are in profound pain because of the death and destruction the Palestinians have had to endure.

Jews see every human being as one of God's children, created in the divine image. Jews dream of a day when all of humanity turns to peace and comes together as one.

It is precisely this idealism that leads many people, including some young Jews, to feel an intuitive sense of compassion for the poor victims of this war.

But compassion should never distort our sense of justice.

There is a strange verse in Exodus 23 which is directed at judges: "You shall not show deference to a poor man in his dispute."

The commentaries are perplexed by this. Generally, it is the powerful, not the poor, who can influence judges and twist judgments. Why is a commandment required to tell judges not to favor the poor?

On this point, many commentaries respond that pious judges may be tempted to distort judgment out of compassion, hoping to give the underdog a leg up.

But there is a further question. The phrasing of this command in Hebrew refers to "deference" which the court might consider giving to the poor person. That seems strange; the verse should have referred to having pity on the poor, which might interfere with judgment. The language of "honoring" the poor seems incongruous; people ordinarily honor the wealthy.

Rabbi David Tzvi Hoffmann notes that the Bible critic Karl August Knobel emended the text and turned the word for poor (*dal*) into great (*gadol*) But well before Knobel confronted this problem, Rabbi Abraham, the son of Maimonides, offered a thoughtful solution. He explains that some assume misery implies a noble goodness. Poverty is thought of as proof of virtue. One might be tempted to assume that the underdog is always right.

This is why Israel faces a unique challenge; in the court of public opinion, those who are strong are assumed to be wrong. Might makes for moral failure. Those who wear the laurels of victimhood best deserve the sympathy of the world.

Because of these unconscious assumptions, the IDF is maligned; even allies engage in a perfunctory denunciation of Israeli excesses.

Some newspaper reporters have become advocates for Hamas, and turn every bit of data into an indictment of Israel. To quote *Alice in Wonderland*, these journalists practice the method of "sentence first, verdict afterward."

But the evidence shows otherwise. John Spencer, chair of urban warfare studies at the Modern War Institute at West Point, wrote that: "In my opinion Israel has implemented more measures to prevent civilian casualties in urban warfare than any other military in the history of war."

Spencer points out the multiple measures Israel has used to diminish civilian casualties, including the use of air-dropped flyers to give instructions on evacuations, radio and social media messages, phone calls and texts to civilians, and roof-knocking (which Spencer points out that "no military has ever implemented in war").

A quick comparison to the battle in Mosul from October 2016 to July 2017 is instructive. The US coalition attacked ISIS in an urban area slightly less densely populated than Gaza, which resulted in the killing of 2,500 ISIS fighters. However, this battle resulted in somewhere between 5,000 and 11,000 civilian deaths. This ratio of civilian to military deaths is anywhere between 2:1 and 4:1. Currently, the ratio in Gaza is 1.8:1.

Spencer is right about the IDF.

Death is always horrible. And all the data in the world will not overcome the tragedy of dead children. And that is what Hamas has been hoping for; they take their own civilians and use them as human shields, and hope that by doing so, the world will prevent Israel from fighting back.

It is here where the calls for a ceasefire begin. But they are generally an exercise in moral condescension. Those who live comfortably in America and have nothing to lose counsel a country that has everything to lose to be patient and lay down their arms in the face of a depraved, bloodthirsty enemy. Sinwar and other Hamas leaders have vowed to repeat October 7th again and again until they destroy Israel. We must take them at their word. To ask Israel, in the name of a phony peace, to allow Hamas to regroup and attack again is suicidal.

Jews know better; empty moral gestures are actually immoral. In 1938, Mahatma Gandhi wrote the following to the head of the German Jewish community, Rabbi Leo Baeck: "My advice to German Jews would be that they commit suicide on a single day, at a single hour. Then would the conscience of Europe awake."

Baeck gave a blunt response: "We Jews know that the single most important commandment of God is to live."

For Jews, pacifism is immoral, because we have a responsibility to care for our own lives and defend ourselves. Rashi in our Torah reading cites the well-known Talmudic rule that "one who comes to kill you, you kill them first." There is a holy obligation to defend our own lives, our own children, and our own country.

Yet this is a very painful obligation. Israel sends its best and brightest to the front lines; and far too many have fallen in battle.

But there is no choice. Cowardice in the face of evil surrenders the world to the wicked. The young men and women in Israel put their lives on the line for the sacred task of protecting the good.

Hamas fights because they hate those who stand before them; the IDF fights because they love those who stand behind them. And that is why the soldiers of the IDF are our heroes.

I recently read a short post about Capt. Rotem Levi, who fell in battle in December. His aunt sent this story to Sivan Rahav Meir, who shared it on her social media accounts.

During the Shiva for Rotem, a comrade of Rotem's explained that one night during battle, when they were together, this soldier couldn't turn on his lightstick, and in frustration called out "enough, what do you want! Everything here is darkness."

Rotem, with absolute calm, said "Turn around. Do you see Nir Oz? (A kibbutz in the Gaza envelope that was attacked.) This is our light, this is what brings us light."

Rotem knew why he was on the front lines; he could turn around and see exactly what he was fighting for. I am heartbroken that this great man had to give up his life to protect Israel. But even in the darkest stretch of Gaza, he kept his eye on what matters: his people, his country. He was thinking of all of us right before he lost his life.

And that is why we are visiting army bases. When the rest of the world turns its back on IDF, we will be there for them. We will tell our beloved soldiers that we stand with Rotem, and we stand with the IDF.

And we tell the world that Rotem was a hero; that they are all our heroes.

Kindness, Freedom, and Victory
Terumah / February 17

Sermon given at The Great Synagogue of Jerusalem, Parshat Terumah.

There is a Chasidic tradition that every Torah reading contains hints regarding the events and news of that week. The Lubavitcher Rebbe referred to this idea frequently, and it can be found in Rabbinic writings as early as the 1600s.

This morning we read Parshat Terumah, and I would like to share my personal connection to this week's Torah reading.

I am in Israel as part of a mission of nearly 50 people from Congregation Kehilath Jeshurun in New York. After spending a week here, it was obvious that this verse at the beginning of the Torah reading reflected our experience: "Speak to the children of Israel, that they bring Me an offering. From everyone who gives it willingly from their heart, you shall take My offering."

Now is a time of great distress and difficulty; the agony of the October 7th massacre is compounded by the continuing tragedy of a painful, grinding war.

Yet against this bleak, dark background, there are a myriad of points of light, beautiful acts of courage and kindness. So many people have stepped forward and are giving from the heart.

There is a *balagan* of courage and kindness. We met a soldier in his 30s who was living with his family in India and operated several businesses there. He flew back immediately to join the battle against Hamas and was seriously injured in battle. Yet he was proud of having fought for his country, and spoke passionately about a communal project in Israel he was planning.

In the Galilee, we met Asma, a Druze woman whose late husband was an IDF soldier who fell in battle. After the war started, she turned her restaurant kosher so she could supply Jewish soldiers with meals. She often gives soldiers meals for free, paying the costs out of her own pocket.

These acts of kindness are bringing very different people closer together. At Hatzalah, we heard about Yossi, a Chasidic volunteer who, along with two friends, rushed out of synagogue on October 7th and drove an ambulance down to the Nova Festival. After completing several hospital transfers, they were transporting a young woman, who complained that she was very cold in the ambulance. Yossi and his team had already used up all the ambulance's blankets, so Yossi reached into the front seat, took his Tallit, and covered the young woman with it. The Nova Festival is worlds apart from Yossi's Chasidic *shtiebel*; but on that day they were united as one.

Never before has a Tallit accomplished such a holy task.

Despite all the distress and difficulty around us, we were buoyed by the remarkable kindness we saw; and as I reread Parshat Terumah last week, I understood it differently.

This year, the chronology of these donations jumped out at me; the newly freed slaves offered these gifts just a short time after the Exodus. Moses didn't need to call for voluntary donations in order to gather the requisite resources for building the sanctuary; the far simpler method of making an assessment, in which each person is taxed, could have accomplished the same thing. (This method would eventually be used with the half-shekel levy in the following Parsha.)

I would argue that the voluntary donations served a larger purpose. Giving is a critical step on the road to freedom, and these donations were instituted to retrain the former slaves.

Several Rabbis have made a similar observation about the Passover Haggadah. The Haggadah begins with *ha lachma anya*, a section that symbolically invites in guests. Why is this the starting point of the Haggadah? Both Rabbi Joseph B. Soloveitchik and Rabbi Jonathan Sacks explain that slaves don't invite guests. Rabbi Soloveitchik simply notes that slaves can't give to others because they have no property of their own; whatever they have belongs to their master. Rabbi

Sacks explains that slaves are self-absorbed, overwhelmed by their day-to-day needs. "Sharing food is the first act through which slaves become free human beings. Someone who fears tomorrow does not offer their bread to others." Giving is a milestone of freedom, a clear sign that one is no longer an anxious slave.

I would take this connection in a different direction, and say that generosity is not just an outcome of freedom; it actually creates the mindset of freedom. A slave is a slave so long as they think like a victim, and a victim cannot figure out how to help themselves, let alone help others. Altruism changes one's self-image—to help others is heroic behavior. Generosity, no matter what the circumstances, allows a person to grab hold of their own destiny.

On our mission, one of the most powerful meetings we had was with Lahav, a special forces veteran who was at the Nova festival with his younger brother. During that day, Lahav nearly lost his life multiple times; his brother was injured. Finally, they managed to escape and get home. The next day, while still in shock, Lahav received a message that he was being called up.

Lahav certainly didn't have to report for duty, but he did anyway. Lahav told us that he realized he needed to flip the narrative; instead of being the victim, he was going to grab hold of his destiny and serve his country.

The next day Lahav was in Kfar Aza, fighting Hamas.

Flipping the narrative is precisely why charity is a critical step on the road to freedom; one becomes a giver, and no longer sees themselves as helpless and needy. That is why this act of communal generosity in Parshat Terumah is so critical for the former slaves.

And today, the charity we saw in Israel speaks of a Jewish spirit that refuses to play the victim.

But this verse also hints at a second insight: charity can teach us a great deal about authentic strength and power.

The Torah portion speaks of the *nediv lev*, one who is giving of their heart; they have a heart that is virtually dripping with goodness. This stands in contrast with Pharaoh's heart, one which is *kaved*, hard, and *chazak*, strong.

Which heart should triumph? One might think the heartless, like Pharaoh, hold the advantage. Actually, the opposite is true. Strength without solidarity fails in the long term.

One of the most difficult visits our group made was to the Shurah army base, which had the grim task of preparing for burial the bodies of the 1,200 people murdered on October 7th. Here, dedicated volunteers from the Chevra Kadisha (burial society) have restored dignity to the dead and offered comfort to their families. Their actions have sanctified this base, which is truly the gates of heaven.

Noa, the head of the women's Chevra Kadisha, explained "I am also fighting Hamas. When we do good, we fight Hamas."

In this short phrase, Noa offered a powerful insight into this parsha: a giving heart is stronger than a heavy, hardened heart. Hardened hatreds can cause a great deal of destruction in explosive bursts of violence, but long-lasting communities require trust, solidarity, and compassion. The *nediv lev* will always outlast the hard-hearted.

This will be true of this war as well. Yahya Sinwar hides in tunnels safe from the very war he set in motion; he uses his people as human shields and cares very little for them. What we saw in Israel was the opposite. People putting others first. People giving from the heart. People standing up for each other.

In Israel we saw that there is nothing as strong as a people united for each other.

And that is the power of the *nediv lev.*

An Ever-Present Void

Tetzaveh / February 23

Moses is not mentioned in Parshat Tetzaveh, the only such instance in the last four books of the Torah. This point, first mentioned by the Baal HaTurim, is a favorite of elementary school teachers looking for fun facts and pulpit rabbis looking for sermon topics.

On its own, this observation is purely an exercise in poetry; in reality, multiple factors determine the division of Torah readings, and the fact that one short Parsha ended up without Moses's name is not all that strange.

What does matter is not whether Moses is "missing" from the Parsha, but our perception of it. The fact that this question is constantly repeated says a great deal about the reader; Moses is not mentioned, and it's noticed.

Even when Moses is gone, he leaves behind a void.

Many of those who comment on Moses's absence relate it to his date of death, which according to the Talmud was on the seventh of Adar; and most years, Tetzaveh and the seventh of Adar are on the same week. (This year they are a week apart.)

The seventh of Adar is included on a list of fast days compiled by the Baal Halakhot Gedolot, an 8th-century work. While these fasts have long fallen out of practice (Rabbi Yoseph Karo writes they had already been discontinued by the 15th century), the fast of the seventh of Adar continued to be practiced by burial societies (Chevra Kadishas). They would assemble together for morning services and recite special selichot prayers about the tasks of a Chevra Kadisha. At night, they would join together for a special meal in honor of their service to the community.

The connection between Chevra Kadishas and Moses is twofold. First, Moses was buried in an unmarked grave by God Himself. In each burial, the Chevra Kadisha follows in God's footsteps, and does a true act of kindness. (Because Moses' grave is unknown, the Israeli rabbinate has also designated the seventh of Adar as the memorial day for soldiers whose burial places are unknown; and there are too many such soldiers from the current war.)

The second reason is that Moses himself is a role model for Chevra Kadishas; as the Jews left Egypt, Moses made certain to take with him Joseph's bones for burial in Israel. Even 400 years later, Joseph's bones were not seen as a funerary relic of the distant past; he was seen as family. And this is the very mission that every Chevra Kadisha is tasked with: to ensure that those who are gone are never forgotten and receive a proper burial.

It is a profoundly holy task. On our missions to Israel, we visited the Shurah Army Base, where the bodies of the 1,200 people murdered on October 7th were processed for burial. The scenes that played out there in the first few days of the war were gut-wrenching. Rabbi Benzi Mann, who has been serving at Shurah since October 7th, spoke about how every refrigerated truck in the country, including dairy transports covered with advertisements for chocolate milk and yogurt, were conscripted to transport bodies; to this day he feels uneasy seeing dairy trucks on the highway. When Benzi would open the trucks' doors, there were so many bodies piled up that blood would come pouring out.

But despite the traumatic circumstances, these incredible reservists worked day and night to ensure the dead got a proper burial, and their families had a chance to wish their loved ones farewell. The dedicated Chevra Kadisha at Shurah did everything possible to treat the dead, and their families, with love.

Rabbi Mann related a conversation between Rabbi Ephraim Mirvis, the Chief Rabbi of England, and President Isaac Herzog of Israel; Rabbi Mirvis told President Herzog he had visited Shurah. President Herzog replied that it was an awful place, "the gates of hell"; the very imprint of Hamas's depraved crimes was on the body of every person murdered.

Rabbi Mirvis responded that on the contrary, Shurah was the "gates of heaven," and a place of awe; it was a place where holy volunteers had heroically restored dignity to the deceased and their families.

The task of the Chevra Kadisha is to ensure that a body is treated with respect. In preparation for burial, they do what is called *taharah* to clean the body and purify it, and recite prayers for the soul of the deceased. (In the case of those murdered on October 7th, many of the usual procedures were suspended; murder victims are meant to be buried in their clothes. However, the prayers and the arrangement of the bodies in the coffin remain the same.) Other societies may cremate remains, or toss them away; Tibetans practice a "sky-burial," in which bodies are placed on the mountaintop to be eaten by vultures. Judaism takes a different view, and sees treating the body with respect as the highest priority.

The Chatam Sofer explains that the *taharah* procedures are to show respect for man, who is created in the "image of God." Even a dead body continues to carry a reflection of the divine image. The Chatam Sofer reminds us that by offering proper respect for the dead body, one offers respect for the living.

Jewish funerary and mourning rituals are not about closure and putting the loss behind us. On the contrary, they are about preserving our connection to those who have passed away. We want to build a bridge from this world to the next, to continue to keep our loved ones in our hearts.

This is what Avishai Margalit has called "the ethics of memory". While the philosophical basis of this idea is complex, it is very much a part of the Jewish tradition. The ritual of Shiva and the prayers of Yizkor and Kaddish all articulate the same idea: we must continue to remember those whom we love. We remember, because to love someone is to love someone forever; we remember because we could never forgive ourselves for forgetting.

On the last day of our most recent mission, we visited Har Herzl, Israel's military cemetery. Two sections have been designated for this war's fallen soldiers. We went on a rainy day and it seemed like the stones were crying. All around us were the graves of people in their twenties and thirties, who once had a bright future ahead of them. A young widow, married for just two months, was sitting next to her husband's grave; he was 23 years old. Our guide Michal spoke about the soldiers she knew in the section, who were friends from her neighborhood and school. Michal is far too young, and should not know such tragedy, but now she does. Like every Israeli, she has gone to shiva after shiva, comforting and bereaved all at once.

On Har Herzl, this overwhelming sense of loss, this endless void, is most profound. There is no grief like the grief of losing a young child at the height of their potential.

But at the same time, there is a recognition that within this absence those who have died will be ever-present. Virtually every grave was decorated by the families in tribute to their loved ones. Bottles of scotch, Israeli flags, soccer flags, photographs, letters, and miniature Torah scrolls. They are declarations that the fallen will never be forgotten. At every simcha, every Seder, every family get-together, they will be remembered. There may be a gaping void in the mourners' hearts, but within that void, the memories of their loved ones are ever-present.

The Bible says "Put me like a seal over your heart, like a seal on your arm. For love is as strong as death." These bereaved families have declared that their love is forever, tied to the heart with an eternal bond. Nothing, not even death, can take their love away.

They will always remember them. And so will we.

May their memory be for a blessing.

Too Soon for Humor?

Purim / March 7

Since October 7th, the Jewish community has been in mourning. Grief is a narrow-minded emotion, with little room for much else, and there certainly is no room for humor. And yet, even in the worst of times, people have to laugh; it's more or less instinctive.

Daniel Gordis wrote about a conversation he had:

> We were coming out of Minchah yesterday afternoon, and the sky had darkened considerably in the very short time we'd been inside. .. I said to a friend who was standing next to me, "What's with the clouds? Is it going to rain? I thought it was supposed to be clear this week."
>
> "No," he said, "Cloudy with a chance of war."
>
> I burst out laughing, as did he. It was hilarious. But also not.

This sort of laughter feels transgressive. We are torn, wondering if it is insensitive to make jokes, both in general, and about this horrible war. In November, an article in Yediot Achronot asked: *Are we allowed to laugh yet?*

A quick glance at Jewish sources yields an unequivocal no. Halakha employs a rigid etiquette that separates joy and grief. It is unseemly if mourners are jovial during shiva; the Talmud writes, "Rav Pappa said...A mourner should not place a young child in their lap because the child will bring them to laughter, and they will be disgraced in the eyes of other people because they laughed while in mourning."

In another passage, the Talmud goes further, requiring everyone to practice self-denial to connect to the communal pain, and says: Reish Lakish said: "It is prohibited for a person to have conjugal relations in years of famine."

Yet these proscriptions don't always fit ordinary life. (For this reason, later halakhic commentaries often treat these passages as general guidance rather than an absolute religious obligation.) Laughter is found in the darkest moments, and tears at the peak of joy; most people can't separate their emotions into neat little compartments, to be pulled out at will when needed. As Gordis realized that afternoon, laughter can arrive without an invitation.

"Hogan's Heroes" was a popular television show when I was young. It was a sitcom about the escapades in a Nazi P.O.W. camp, where the prisoners constantly fooled the hapless Germans. Even as a child, I was bewildered by the show; in reality the Nazis were brutal and efficient, nothing like the characters on Hogan's Heroes. Later I learned that four of the characters on the show, including those of the three senior Nazis, were played by Jewish refugees from Europe; the parents of Leon Askin, who played the German General Albert Hans Burkhalter on the show, were murdered in Treblinka. This was even more confounding; how could Jewish refugees play Nazis on TV, just 20 years after the war?

While the line between bad taste and good comedy is elusive, Hogan's Heroes may have landed on the wrong side of what is appropriate. But perhaps a partial defense of this bizarre show can be offered by Robert Clary, who played Corporal LeBeau, a French P.O.W. Clary was a survivor of Buchenwald, who lost his parents and 10 of his siblings during the Holocaust. When he reflected on his experiences later in life, he said his ability to sing, to laugh, and to entertain enabled him to survive. Yes, a good joke can sometimes be the difference between life and death; and during the Holocaust, many used jokes as a tool of survival.

Several books and articles have been written about Holocaust humor, and a number of the jokes have been preserved. (One example: "Every day in the ghetto is like a holiday. We sleep in a Sukkah, dress up like it's Purim, and eat like it's Yom Kippur.") The most thorough academic study of this phenomenon is Itamar Levin's Hebrew work *Through the Tears*. In his introduction, Levin writes about the different purposes of humor. Sometimes it is the "weapon of the weak," who got a measure of retribution by mocking their Nazi tormentors. But the larger purpose was to preserve people's sanity when insanity was the natural reaction, and to give people hope when everything looked hopeless.

Rabbi Jonathan Sacks once offered a comment critical of Roberto Benigni's "Life is Beautiful," a film about how a father saved his son's life during the Holocaust by making jokes. Rabbi Sacks wrote that he disagreed with the film's thesis that humor can keep you alive. After a speech, a Holocaust survivor approached Sacks to correct him on this point. Rabbi Sacks writes:

> "You are wrong," ...(he) said to me, and then, he told me his story. He and another prisoner in Auschwitz had become friends. They reached the conclusion that unless they were able to laugh, they would eventually lose the will to live. So they made an agreement. Each of them would look out, every day, for something about which they could laugh. Each night they would share their findings and laugh together. "A sense of

humor," said the survivor, looking me in the eyes, "kept me alive."

Sacks then realized that these Holocaust jokes could be heroic and life-sustaining. Reflecting on this later, he wrote: "I cannot say I understand such courage, but I found it awe-inspiring."

The Halakhic proscriptions against joy in times of grief are quite meaningful; they emphasize the moral obligation to mourn the death of a beloved relative. These rules are necessary because sometimes a Shiva house can feel like a party, with copious food and chatter about golf games and vacations.

However, even at the worst of times, joy must never disappear. Chasidic thinkers have stressed how central joy is to one's religious identity. This emphasis is not just because of joy's spiritual importance; recognizing the enormous pain Jews carried from years of exile, the Chasidic masters saw happiness and laughter as the way to heal long-standing psychic wounds.

Even Tisha B'Av, the most tragic day on the Jewish calendar, is recast as a time of joy. First, there is the extraordinary explanation of the Chozeh (Seer) of Lublin to the Talmudic phrase "when the month of Av enters, one reduces joy." This is ordinarily understood as meaning that one must already diminish joy nine days before Tisha B'av. The Chozeh had a dramatic rereading of this text; he read it as meaning that when the dark month of Av arrives, one diminishes the pain of the month by adding joy! This idea was reflected in practice as well. Some Chasidic Jews had the custom to play pranks on each other on Tisha B'Av; oftentimes it was the children throwing *berelach*, little brambles during Kinot to lighten up the mood. Chasidic leaders felt that the Jews in Eastern Europe had lived with too much distress and that a painful Tisha B'Av would do more harm than good.

A similar insight is offered regarding the corresponding phrase "When the month of Adar arrives, we increase joy." The Sefat Emet notes that Adar is the month that is repeated in a leap year (such as this year) when there is a doubling of the month of joy. This, he explains, underlines the centrality of joy; and Jews need as much joy as they get.

Purim this year will be different. A tragic war is still ongoing; much like Av, it will be difficult to laugh. Yet at the same time we need to find a way to lift our spirits, to find that double portion of joy that two Adars bring.

I am a big fan of the Israel sketch comedy show *Eretz Nehederet*. One of the recurring sketches is of Asher Ben Chorin (Yuval Semo), who is a parody of the average Israeli taxi driver who says outlandish things to his passengers. (The passengers are all in on the joke before they enter the car.) One of the segments in November was exceptional. Semo was driving evacuees from the communities near Gaza in his taxi. He started with his ordinary jokes, talking about how being an evacuee is now a "status," and remarking to one couple, who were being housed in the Royal Beach Hotel, "that when I was on my honeymoon I didn't go to such a good hotel." To Tomer and Guy, two young men from Kfar Aza, he says "you should consider moving to somewhere calmer—maybe Dagestan" before declaring that what was really needed "is to rebrand Kfar Aza and give it a different name—like *Neveh Steinman*."

But then the conversations changed in tone. He takes Noa, a young mother of three from Sufa, who explains that her husband went out that morning to defend their Kibbutz and never returned. Yes, there are jokes in their conversation; when he asks Noa how her kids are, she says "annoying, as always." She explains that she will return to Sufa because it was her husband's birthplace and home, and that is where they belong. The conversation ends in tears and a hug.

In his conversation with Tomer and Guy, Tomer tells Semo that both his parents, Ram and Lily, were murdered. Semo says that for the first time in 30 years, he is at a loss for words. Tomer continues, and says that his sister said it is almost a month since their parents' deaths, and Tomer needed to smile; that is why he signed up to be on the show. And then Tomer adds that it had been his father's dream to be in Semo's taxi sketch. This poignant moment continues with a conversation about Tomer's parents, before ending with Semo wisecracking "Don't think I'm not going to charge you for this ride."

From beyond the tears, these gentle jokes honor Ram and Lily, and Tomer and Guy's smiles carry their legacy. Sometimes, laughter is the right way to grieve; and their tears and smiles combine to leave them stronger.

This Purim we too will laugh and cry; and both the smiles and the tears will honor the legacy of the fallen. Laughter has helped the Jewish people survive. Joy sits at the center of the Jewish soul.

And that is why it is never too soon for Purim, never too soon for a joke.

The Day After
Pekudei / March 14

Every ending is a new beginning.

When we conclude each of the Five Books of the Torah (as we will this week), the reader leads the congregation in the refrain "*chazak chazak v'nitchazek*," "be strong, be strong, and be strengthened."

This custom began in the 1100s and is one of a group of customs related to finishing a Torah reading. Sephardic custom is that after one receives an aliyah, other people greet them with "*chazak u'baruch* — may you be strong and blessed"; Ashkenazi Jews say instead "*yiyasher kochacha* — may your strength be renewed." In other words, you can't coast after a success, after completing a section; you need to stay strong. Similarly, after finishing an entire book of the Talmud, we read the *siyum* declaration which begins with the words "*hadran alach*," "I will return to you," expressing a commitment to review what was just studied. These customs declare that one can never retire from responsibility, even after extraordinary success. Endings are never the end.

For the same reason, on Simchat Torah, when we read the final Torah reading of the year, we go a step further and start reading the Torah again from the beginning. We want to make it clear we are not going to abandon the Torah, once completed. (Rabbi Joseph Ber Soloveitchik suggests that this may be why we say Adon Olam at the end of the Musaf prayer on Shabbat morning; even after lengthy service, we go right back to the very first prayer, indicating we are ready to start all over again!)

Every victory brings with it the possibility of a letdown. Overconfidence can turn strong armies into weak ones. It is precisely after achieving success, after concluding the task, that we have to remember to "be strong, be strong, and be strengthened."

One of the major British victories in World War II was the second Battle of El-Alamein, which ended on November 11, 1942. That day, Winston Churchill spoke to the Parliament to report on the victory. Then he added the following:

> We are entitled to rejoice only upon the condition that we do not relax. I always liked those lines by the American poet, Walt Whitman. I have several times repeated them. They apply today most aptly. He said: "...Now understand me well—it is provided in the essence of things that from any fruition of success, no matter what, shall come forth something to make a greater struggle necessary." The problems of victory are

more agreeable than those of defeat, but they are no less difficult. ...We shall need to use the stimulus of victory to increase our exertions, to perfect our systems, and to refine our processes.

This is an eloquent restatement of "*chazak chazak v'nitchazek.*" Unlike the tagline of the beer ads, after a task is complete, it is not "Miller Time." Victory brings with it a multitude of problems, and the greatest of them all is being spoiled by success.

Every new chapter requires an even greater struggle.

The catastrophe of October 7th occurred due to the sins of overconfidence. Multiple warnings were ignored, while the political and military leadership clung to the assumption that the enemy simply would not attack despite clear evidence otherwise. No one remembered the lesson of "*chazak chazak v'nitchazek.*"

In retrospect, this war will probably be seen as a defeat and victory mashed up together much like the Yom Kippur War 50 years ago. Now, what happens the "day after" has been discussed, almost from the very beginning. Pundits, politicians, and polemicists all offer their visions. They are planning for a very different political and social landscape.

While a new blueprint is probably necessary, even more important than that is a new mindset.

History is considered by Judaism as a form of revelation. In a recent seminar, I made mention of Emil Fackenheim's "614th commandment." Fackenheim was a prolific writer on the theology of the Holocaust and believed that history is a form of revelation. The Holocaust, he argued, despite its horrors, carries the commanding voice of history. To Fackenheim, this voice declared: "Thou shalt not hand Hitler posthumous victories." That is a new commandment, the 614th commandment. One of his students paraphrased Fackenheim's four-fold view of this commandment as meaning: "Jews must remain Jews, they must remember the Shoah victims, they must not despair of man, and they must not despair of God."

History as revelation is the very lesson of Purim. Megilat Esther meticulously excludes mentioning God's name. Instead, it urges us to hear God through the commanding voice of history. Much like Fackenheim's understanding, the practical commandments in Megilat Esther offer a series of lessons as well, which I would summarize this way:

> Evil exists. Celebrate salvation, and celebrate with friends. Care for the vulnerable. Connect to your community.

Read aloud these lessons every year so you don't forget them.

The lessons of history cannot offer a blueprint for the future; circumstances change all the time. Instead, they are meant to transform our perspective, to allow us to meet the challenges of the future.

After October 7th, a commanding voice calls out to us again, asking us to see the world differently. Bret Stephens, in a brilliant column, wrote that:

> "There used to be a sign somewhere in the C.I.A.'s headquarters that read, "Every day is Sep. 12." It was placed there to remind the agency's staffers that what they felt right after the attacks of September 11, 2001 — the sense of outrage and purpose, of favoring initiative over caution, of taking nothing for granted — had to be the mind-set with which they arrived to work every day.
>
> There ought to be a similar sign in every Jewish organization, synagogue, and day school, and on the desks of anyone — Jewish or not — for whom the

security and well-being of the Jews is a sacred calling: "Every day is Oct. 8.""

This is a powerful point. Jews must nevermore be naive. Our destiny can no longer depend on here today, gone tomorrow "allies," and our security must depend on something more than a high-tech fence.

But the voice of history has much more to say about October 7th. One day a megillah of October 7th will be composed, and contain all the horrible stories of tragedy, as well as the inspiring stories of unity, heroism, and optimism. And through these stories, we will hear God's commanding voice, and learn lessons about the mindset we need in order to move forward into the future.

Allow me to share one such story. This past week I met a young woman from Kfar Aza, Or Tzuk, who spoke at an AIPAC conference.

On October 7th, Hamas terrorists murdered her parents. Her 25-year-old brother was able to survive by hiding under a bed; he stayed there for seven hours just inches from his own mother's body, soaked in her blood. (Or and her husband had gone away on vacation.)

Or told us how she promised her brother that whatever happens in the future, she will always care for him; he can come any day and move right into her house. And she told everyone that she was three months pregnant, and had thrown up just before she got on stage.

When I spoke to her afterward, I asked Or why she decided to get pregnant just two months after her parents were brutally murdered. Her response was simple; Jews know they must choose life. Jews must always be optimistic, even in the worst of times.

Or said she drew inspiration from the Jewish holidays. Unlike many other cultures and religions, Jewish holidays are not unvarnished stories of joy; rather, they tell stories about how resilient heroes like Esther, Moses, and the Maccabees overcame extreme challenges.

When speaking to Or, I realized that I was talking to a modern-day Esther. She has heard a voice calling out, telling her to choose life, to choose family, to choose community.

And that voice speaks to us too. This is the only way forward on the day after.

The Sacrifices of Others
Tzav / March 28

Amitai Granot died on October 7th when Hezbollah fired missiles at Israeli positions in the North. He was engaged to be married.

His father, Rabbi Tamir Granot, is the Rosh Yeshiva of Ohr Shaul, which is in South Tel Aviv. He is a brilliant Torah scholar who wrote a Ph.D. on religious responses to the Holocaust.

On October 26th, I visited with Rabbi Granot at his yeshiva. In the course of our conversation, he explained that searching for meaning helped him cope with the death of his son. In an article he wrote at the time, he explained that "the way to deal with a period of difficult crisis like the present is never to blame, retreat into oneself, or despair, but rather to believe, hope, think only positive thoughts, seek out the good in people, and to find ways to act, save, help, and fix."

And that is what he has been doing since October 7th. In particular, Rabbi Granot has focused on "the day after the war," and bringing Israel's diverse factions closer together in the future.

Right before Hamas attacked, there were acute divisions over judicial reform, which divided right from left, religious from secular. Rabbi Granot recognizes that Israel can never return to the resentments and divisions of October 6th if she wants to survive.

After observing shiva for his son, Rabbi Granot immediately arranged meetings with a diverse group of religious and political leaders. His message to them was that they must learn how to understand each other's worlds and appreciate the sacrifice each group makes for Jewish survival.

When I saw him in October, he felt his message was being listened to carefully. At that point, the country had come together in never-before-seen solidarity; significant ideological and political differences were put aside for the greater good. Non-kosher restaurants were turning Kosher in order to feed religious soldiers, and ultra-Orthodox organizations were bringing supplies to evacuees from thoroughly secular kibbutzim.

Recently, this unity has begun to shrink and shrivel; even with a war still raging on several fronts, old animosities have returned.

In the last few weeks, one issue that worried Rabbi Granot deeply has reappeared: the exemption of yeshiva (rabbinical school) students from military service. Right now, the government needs to introduce new legislation before this exemption, which was long ago struck down by the Supreme Court, expires on March 31st.

The debate over military service is often seen as part of the secular/religious divide, but that mischaracterizes the reality. From the very beginning of the state, there has been a heated debate within the religious community about army service. In 1948, one of Israel's leading Rabbis, Shlomo Yosef Zevin, wrote an anonymous letter protesting the refusal of the Roshei Yeshiva (Yeshiva deans) to send their students to war. He felt it was an embarrassment that the greatest Torah scholars had ignored their own community's obligation to defend the State. At the beginning of the letter he points out that saving lives is the highest responsibility in Judaism; if so, the pious should be first in line to take on army service.

In an agitated tone, Rabbi Zevin challenged his colleagues:

> "And you, our great masters, most of you admit the dire necessity of this necessary war....therefore, it is your obligation to encourage even Torah scholars, those young and healthy enough to go into battle, to do so. "Will you send your brothers to war, and yourselves sit at home?"""

Rabbi Zevin's argument is from an insider, directed at other insiders. He argues that the exemption of yeshiva students from military duty is contrary to Torah values.

Many devoted Torah scholars recognized that both Torah study and military service are critical. The Yeshivot Hesder system was created to allow that possibility; its students spend five years in this intensive dual program, combining army service and yeshiva study. Rabbi Aharon Lichtenstein explained the ethos of Hesder this way:

> "Hesder at its finest seeks to attract and develop bnei torah (Torah students) who are profoundly motivated by the desire to become serious talmidei chachamim (scholars) but who concurrently feel morally and religiously bound to help defend their people and their country; who, given the historical exigencies of their time and place, regard this dual commitment as both a privilege and a duty; who, in comparison with their non-hesder confreres love not (to paraphrase Byron's *Childe Harold*) Torah less but Israel more."

Despite these arguments, the Charedi leadership has remained strenuously opposed to allowing yeshiva students to join the army; currently, 66,000 students are exempted from army service. This has become a social norm, which makes it difficult for those who don't study well to opt out of yeshiva; currently, an estimated 20-30% of registered yeshiva students (and perhaps more) spend little or no time studying. But they remain in yeshiva anyway, instead of serving in the army. To leave yeshiva is considered to be an admission of failure.

Over the years, the issue of drafting yeshiva students has been politicized; as a result, the language used by defenders of the status quo has become harsher and harsher. One major moment of conflict was in 2014; the rhetoric used then by some Charedi opponents of the draft was "The government is going to send yeshiva students to jail for learning Torah." They equated the Israeli government with Czarist Russia in its hatred of Judaism.

That crisis, like many others, passed, and the rhetoric was mostly forgotten; but right now, right in the middle of a war, the issue of drafting yeshiva students has come back. An extension to the yeshiva student draft exemption has expired, and without new legislation, these students will have to report to the army.

In response, harsh rhetoric has exploded again. In a shocking statement about drafting yeshiva students, the Sephardic Chief Rabbi Yitzchak Yoseph, said, "If they force us to join the army, we will all move abroad." This statement was not an outlier; the words used by other religious leaders have been equally inflammatory.

Rabbi Granot was shaken by these words.

In a videotaped talk, he spoke about the importance of each group in Israel learning to respect each other. He repeated, as he has said many a time, that secular Israelis need to have a greater appreciation of how yeshivas are preserving the Jewish tradition. He emphasized that: "And you, our secular brothers, should tell the yeshivot, 'We want yeshivot and we will never harm them. We also wish to learn Torah, in our own way, and we will defend and support yeshivot—if you will be our partners.'"

He had redoubled his efforts to dialogue and unity since his son's death, and he has not left that commitment.

But he is also the father of a fallen soldier. And in a pained voice, Rabbi Granot turned to Rabbi Yitzchak Yoseph and said:

> "...Your words about drafting yeshiva students caused my wife to cry for 24 hours straight. I wish to open my remarks with her tears—the tears of the mother of my son, Capt. Amitai Granot z"l, who was killed five months ago in the battle against Hezbollah. Amitai

was a 24-year-old yeshiva student, he learned for three years in yeshiva, he enlisted and was an officer; he deeply wished to return to his learning in yeshiva. He loved the Torah to the very depths of his soul....

On behalf of my wife, Avivit, Amitai's mother, I ask you, Honorable Rabbi, in the name of her tears: Am I wrong? Is it in vain that our son now rests in a grave on Mount Herzl? Should he, and all his friends buried alongside him, have remained in their yeshivot, delegating to secular citizens the duty of mesirut nefesh, ultimate sacrifice? Perhaps they should have gone abroad to study Torah and to avoid enlisting?.....

Honorable Rabbi, you should seek forgiveness from my wife, from her tears, and you should go up to Mount Herzl and ask forgiveness from Amitai z"l, a yeshiva student and warrior, and from all the righteous and holy and pure Torah students who choose to fight, as well as from the soldiers who do not study Torah—all of whom gave their lives in defense of our nation and those who dwell in it. Is it reasonable to leave the Holy Land to avoid defending it in a milchemet mitzvah (necessary war) for the salvation of the entire nation? Are we in the Russian Empire? Is this the Czar's army? Are Jewish boys being dragged off as cantonists?"

In this pained *cri de coeur*, Rabbi Granot exposes the greatest obstacle to building unity for the future. On October 7th, when the future of the State of Israel hung by a thread, it was soldiers like Amitai Granot z"l who saved the lives of every Israeli citizen, including, of course, every yeshiva student. And so many like Amitai have lost their lives; since October 7th, 597 soldiers have given their lives in defense of the State of Israel.

What disturbed Rabbi Granot most about these statements was the profound lack of appreciation for military service. Rabbis like Yitzchak Yoseph were treating service in the IDF as a calamity, one so awful it would make sense to move to another country; the disrespect for every soldier, as well as the young men and women buried on Har Herzl, is implicit.

The way forward on this issue is fraught with difficulty; some compromise will be proposed and debated, and then another. At some point the process will end. But sadly, this may lay the ground for future conflict, because achieving unity through compromise is no simple task. Often, people are angrier after compromising, with a sense of buyer's remorse; they are left feeling they have given up too much and gotten back too little.

The only way to an authentic compromise is both sacrifice and appreciation. Rabbi Jonathan Sacks correctly points out that the overarching theme of Vayikra is sacrifice, and explains in his commentary to Parshat Tzav that the ability to sacrifice is critical for society:

> "Lose the concept of sacrifice within a society, and sooner or later marriage falters, parenthood declines, and the society slowly ages and dies. My late predecessor, Lord Jakobovits, had a lovely way of putting this. The Talmud says that when a man divorces his first wife, "the altar sheds tears." What is the connection between the altar and a marriage? Both, he said, are about sacrifices. Marriages fail when the partners are unwilling to make sacrifices for one another."

I would add one point to what Lord Rabbi Jakobovits said. If we don't appreciate the sacrifices of others, relationships will fail as well. Every good relationship requires both sacrifice and a true appreciation for the sacrifice of others.

This lesson is more critical than ever for Israel, which is once again descending into paralyzing dysfunction.

It's time for all of Israel to appreciate the sacrifices of others.

The Death of a Child, the Love for Life
Shemini / April 5

There is no tragedy like the death of a child. There is so much grief that it's impossible to communicate one's feelings to others. A couple I once counseled had lost their six-year-old son to a sudden illness. To make matters worse, the tragedy made them feel isolated from their friends, who could still tuck all their children into bed at night. They bitterly explained to me that "there are two types of people in the world: those who have lost a child, and those who have not." As much as their friends (and rabbi) could empathize, they were mourning alone.

After losing two of his sons, Aaron also mourns alone. On the greatest day of his life, the dedication of the sanctuary, (the very day when he and his family are to be inducted into the *Kehunah*, the Jewish priesthood,) Aaron's sons Nadav and Avihu are suddenly struck dead by God.

Aaron has the following conversation with his brother Moses about these deaths.

> And Moses said to Aaron, "This is what the Lord spoke, saying:
>
> 'By those who are close to Me
> I will be sanctified;
> And before all the people
> I will be glorified.' "
>
> And Aaron was silent.

These words are unclear; who are the ones close to God, and how do they sanctify God in the presence of death? Due to its ambiguity, there are many interpretations; but the one offered by the Rashbam and Rabbi Yosef Bechor Shor is the most convincing. They explain that Moses is addressing a difficult question: does Aaron leave the sanctuary in order to mourn, or does he carry on with the special service of the dedication?

Moses's response offers guidance for this situation. He says that those who are close to God, such as the Kohen Gadol (High Priest), must sanctify God by putting their own grief aside and continuing the service. (The Mishnah will codify this into law, that the Kohen Gadol continues to serve in the Temple even when he is a mourner.)

Despite his own heartbreak, Aaron accepts this directive and remains silent, with no tears, no words of eulogy. Yet his silence contains multitudes of emotions too large to articulate in words; quietly, Aaron expresses both endless grief and unwavering determination.

Aaron's silence can still be heard today. Rabbi Hanan Porat lived in Kfar Etzion as a small child in the 1940's. During the battles following U.N. Resolution 181, the Kibbutz was under constant attack. Eventually, the Kibbutz fell into Jordanian hands. Most of the women and children were evacuated from the Kibbutz, while almost all the men died; many were massacred after surrendering to the Arab Legion. After the War of Independence was over, the children of Kfar Etzion were raised on the dream of returning home.

In a commentary on Parshat Shemini, Porat quotes the Rashbam's words, which he interprets as a call to bereaved leaders to put aside their personal grief and continue with their mission. He then explains that the children of Kfar Etzion were raised to understand that, "public emissaries cannot break down when they are beset by a personal crisis, even if it is too heavy to bear, such as the loss of a dear son or a beloved wife. But instead, they need to grit their teeth, hold their silence, and continue with dedication to their national mission."

And so it was. After the Six-Day War, Porat, along with the other children of the Kibbutz, rebuilt Kfar Etzion. They never forgot their mission; and after holding their silence for 19 years, they returned home.

It is heroic to persevere with a broken heart, to look death right in the eye and still hold tight to one's mission. But there is another interpretation of the Rashbam which complements this idea: the sanctity of life.

Rabbi Joseph B. Soloveitchik writes in *Halakhic Man* about Judaism's theology of life. He notes that many religions sanctify death, and see it as the portal to the world to come. Judaism takes a dramatically different approach. It sees death as defilement, the very opposite of holiness. One who comes in contact with a dead body cannot enter the Temple or offer a sacrifice. When a relative dies, we grieve, tear our garments, and sit on the floor, bitterly rejecting death. Holiness is consistently associated with life, which is why we suspend observance of Shabbat, or any other commandment, if there is the slightest concern that it will endanger someone's life.

Judaism is a religion of life.

Rabbi Soloveitchik explains that the Kohen Gadol does not take part in mourning rituals because his role is all-encompassing. Even when elsewhere, the Kohen Gadol is metaphorically always present in the Temple, always attached to the sacred; such a person must always be distant from death.

This gives further depth to the words of the Rashbam: Aaron must continue on with the service, despite his personal bereavement, because his mission is a mission of life. What is heroic must always stand in service of a culture of life. And that lesson is all the more critical today, during this war.

Hamas brutally attacked Israel on October 7th with a degree of sadism unparalleled in recent decades; rapes, torture, beheadings, and burning babies alive. But Hamas is not just interested in murdering Jews. At the time of the attack, Yahya Sinwar and the leaders of Gaza understood that the Israeli counterattack would cause their people enormous misery, but they didn't care. They had long used civilians as human shields, building terror bases in hospitals, setting up rocket launch sites near schools. Civilian casualties are a strategic advantage for Hamas; the deaths of Palestinian civilians lead to greater international pressure on Israel. All too often, Hamas troops try to prevent ordinary Gazans from seeking safe haven during the war.

Hamas leaders repeat the mantra "we love death like our enemies love life," and see the Israeli love for life to be a strategic disadvantage. And Hamas is not completely incorrect. They can divert much-needed supplies into building tunnels and rockets because the lives of Palestinians are not as important as a 100-year war. They also know that in Israel an entire country cares for each hostage, and an entire country cries for each fallen soldier. Israel will make difficult compromises in order to bring her soldiers home to their families and her hostages back to safety.

But the strategic advantage of "loving death" comes with even greater disadvantages. Hamas has embraced a death cult, one that has been ruinous for Gaza. The love of death can become an obsession, driving young people to become "heroic" martyrs, dying in the service of even more death. And this belief that they can defeat Israel by embracing death has led to Hamas's reckless decisions during this war. Love of death will end up being a self-fulfilling aspiration.

Judaism embraces life. And during this war with a death cult, Israelis have embraced life, perhaps even more than before. And that is truly inspiring.

This week, one story in the news touched me profoundly. The family of Sergeant Major Sivan Weil, an IDF soldier who died on Sunday, donated his organs to save the lives of five critically ill Israelis.

His parents made a statement explaining that this "donation helped to perpetuate the memory of our angel." They continued, "Sivan was exceptionally strong with a heart of gold. He saved many people's lives during his military service. We hope his organ donation will continue saving people's lives."

Despite their own grief, they have taken on a mission of kindness. They are emulating Aaron's example, showing incredible courage after the death of a child.

With broken hearts, Sivan's parents are showing us the way forward: life, and only life.

Are We Going to Stop for Lunch?
Pesach / April 11

Jan Karski was among the first to warn the world about the Holocaust. A member of the Polish Underground, Karski courageously went back and forth between German-occupied Poland and the Allied countries. During his missions, he infiltrated several concentration camps and brought word to the world of the horrors he witnessed there. And he was ignored.

This might have shocked Karski, but not the Polish Jews; they had been reaching out every way they could to their brethren in the United States, but to no avail. In 1942, just before he left the Warsaw Ghetto to bring a report to the United States, these Polish Jews explained to Karski that: "Jewish leaders abroad won't be interested. At 11 in the morning you will begin telling them about the anguish of the Jews in Poland, but at 1 o'clock they will ask you to halt the narrative so they can have lunch."

Breaking for lunch is the hard stop of feigned interest, the end of a meeting that was merely for show. The Jews of America didn't care enough to do anything.

When Rabbi Joseph B. Soloveitchik reflected on the American Jewish response, he wrote:

> Let us be honest. During the terrible Holocaust, when European Jewry was

systematically destroyed in gas chambers and crematoria, the American Jewish community did not rise to the occasion.... and we did precious little to save our unfortunate brethren.....

We witnessed the most horrible tragedy in our history, and we were silent.

Jews are obligated to help other Jews. This is far from an obvious idea; no other national group inculcates a similar sense of mutual responsibility. Yet the slogan "all Jews are responsible for one another" is a foundation of Judaism.

The source of this obligation is unclear. Rabbi Shneur Zalman of Liadi wrote that "all Israelites are called actual "brothers" because their souls are rooted together...with only the bodies separated." To be a Jew is to have an innate connection with other Jews; they are always brothers and sisters, even if they are from another family.

Rabbi Soloveitchik takes a non-mystical approach, one rooted in history and halakhah. Jews have a mutual covenant which was established during the exile in Egypt. It is based on shared experiences of persecution and suffering, which have remained a reality for much of Jewish history. Antisemitism doesn't discriminate between Jews;

when one Jew is attacked, every other Jew knows they are vulnerable.

The Covenant of Egypt is a partnership between Jews forged by a collective history. This covenant becomes the foundation of Jewish identity.

We are required to feel the pain and suffering of other Jews. As Rabbi Soloveitchik puts it: "If boiling water is poured on the head of a Moroccan Jew, the prim and proper Jew in Paris or London must scream...."

Jewish unity begins in Egypt. A comment in the *Midrash* sees the Egyptian exile as having a silver lining because it forced all Jews to build bridges. Initially, the sons of Jacob who were born to Rachel and Leah looked down on the sons of the maidservants Bilhah and Zilpah. But after 400 years in Egyptian exile, God says "I will redeem them and give them the Pesach ritual, ...and they will declare, "We were all slaves to Pharaoh." And then all Jews will be equal."

The hidden lesson of Pesach is to remember we were all once slaves, and therefore we must all know each other's pain. When a mob of antisemites chases Jews anywhere, it is a danger to Jews everywhere.

Unity most naturally emerges from uniformity. But now, Jews have become more fragmented and dispersed. Differences in religion, ideology, and culture have made division the new default setting. For the last 200 years, the age-old value of unity is no longer a given.

With each new crisis, what remained to be seen was: would the Jewish community meet the challenge?

During the Holocaust, American Jewry failed; but a few years later, they would step up.

The Soviet Jewry movement began on April 27, 1964, when Yaakov Birnbaum convened the founding meeting of the College Students' Struggle for Soviet Jewry (SSSJ). About 200 people attended the first meeting.

Birnbaum's vision was to start with students organizing protest rallies. Student action would inspire the larger Jewish community to join in the protests, which in turn would pressure the American government to act, and then the American government would pressure the Soviet Union to let the Jews leave. The vision seemed fantastically quixotic at the time, but less than a decade later, tens of thousands of exit visas a year were being granted to Soviet Jews. Birnbaum was right.

Driving Birnbaum was guilt. Just twenty years earlier six million Jews were murdered and American Jews did nothing. Would American Jews fail once again?

In a flyer inviting students to the April 1964 meeting, Birnbaum wrote:

> "A recent visitor to Russia was approached by a man with glowing eyes, who whispered *"Far voos shveigt ir? —* Why do you keep silent?" We, who condemn silence and inaction during the Nazi Holocaust, dare we keep silent now?"

Birnbaum was determined that American Jews would not repeat the mistakes of the past. The Jews of the Soviet Union were in pain, and the Jews of America would scream for them.

Now, in 2024, history turns to us again. So far, the American Jewish community has been exceptional in its support for Israel. But there is a long road ahead, and the question remains: will we continue with this support?

Donor fatigue has started to set in. Fundraising campaigns are scuttled because people don't want to be asked again. This is understandable. There is a certain rhythm to ordinary fundraising; causes make asks once or twice a year, and move on. This year has been different, with a new request for funds on an almost daily basis. I have been told more than once that people have reached their limits. It is certainly exhausting to keep up this level of support.

I cannot contradict this sentiment. There has been exceptional generosity over the last six months, with people giving above and beyond what they have ever done before. How much more can we ask for?

But I think we can change our perspective if we consider two things. First, this war is a marathon, not a sprint; unlike past crises, this conflict will not pass in a matter of weeks or months. Israel will need to keep going. And so will we.

More importantly, we need to recognize the screaming pain our brothers and sisters in Israel are enduring. People's lives have been completely crushed. Rachel Goldberg-Polin, whose son Hersh has been held captive in Gaza for six months, says that every day she "puts on a costume and pretends to be a human." A friend who lost a child in battle months ago refuses to be consoled, unable to find joy in nearly anything. And I hear from parents of soldiers that when their children are on the battlefront in Gaza, they cannot sleep at night, and they jump every time the doorbell rings.

Our fatigue pales in comparison with their pain. And now the challenge put before American Jewry is: Are we going to stop for lunch?

1,600 Yizkors

Pesach Yizkor / May 2

The Frankfurt *Memorbuch* was inaugurated in 1711 after the previous one was burned in a fire. Currently housed at the National Library of Israel, it is an enormous book that weighs nearly 30 pounds, with 5,726 entries, plus multiple prayers written on 1,073 pages of parchment.

Memorbuchs like the one from Frankfurt were once a fixture in many Askenazic synagogues; the earliest extant copy of one, the Nuremberg Memorbuch, was composed in the late 1200s. They listed people who had donated specifically to have prayers recited for their souls after their death. (Sometimes the families of the deceased would offer a posthumous donation to have their relatives listed.) New names would be added on an ongoing basis; on specific Shabbats and Holidays, the book would be read from during the service and prayers recited for those inscribed.

Yet the *Memorbuch* is no historical relic. Yehuda Galinsky has shown that the current Ashkenazic Yizkor service is simply a variation on the Memorbuch prayers; this change, which took place in the 1400s, shifted Yizkor from the prayer leader to the individual congregant, allowing them to pray for whomever they chose to.

Unfortunately, the shift to a personal Yizkor left significant prayers behind. The *Memorbuch* also contained regular prayers for historical figures. This included rabbis such as Rabbeinu Gershom and Rashi, as well as an exhaustive registry of martyrs who had died "al Kiddush Hashem," murdered because they were Jewish.

The Nuremberg *Memorbuch*, as well as all subsequent *Memorbuch*s, contains a lengthy town-by-town list of martyrs from the First Crusade in 1096, the Rintfleisch massacres in the summer of 1298, and the Black Death massacres of 1349. The list includes obscure villages that otherwise have been forgotten to history; but Jews once lived in these places, only to be murdered by their neighbors. In Eggolsheim, five families were killed in 1298; in Niesten and Stubenberg, the Jews of the community were burned to death. The Nuremberg *Memorbuch* is the only remaining memorial to their lives.

The *Memorbuch* transformed the consciousness of Ashkenazic Jewry. Debra Kaplan explains that it created a common heritage for diverse communities, and linked generations together in a shared history. German communities in the early 1900s were still reading the names of those who were martyred in Worms and Mainz 800 years earlier; for them, the names of the past were not part of the past at all.

Collective memory is central to Judaism; the root for memory, *zachor*, appears over 200 times in the

Tanakh. It offers a way of bridging the past and present, for every generation to envision themselves standing alongside their ancestors, reliving their history. But the names and mini-biographies of the *Memorbuch* take this a step further; written in tears, they speak of these massacres with a combination of defiance and love.

Even in the short, terse inscriptions about the early martyrs, one can see the rage bubbling underneath. One such line about the city of Worms tells of "Master Shemaryah who was buried alive, and whose wife, sons, and daughters were slaughtered."

These words cry out for justice. Medieval Jews may have been relatively powerless, but they remained steadfastly proud. The authors of the Memorbuch refused to make peace with the injustice of antisemitism.

And later generations promised that they would remember. The names of the martyrs were repeated in synagogues far and wide, even centuries later. Memory became the vehicle for a communal embrace, an act of tenderness that declared "love is as strong as death."

After the Holocaust, the *Memorbuch* returned. Small groups of survivors worked tirelessly to create *Yizkorbuchs* dedicated to telling the story of the communities destroyed by the Nazis. They felt an intense sense of urgency; they were the only ones who could still tell the story. Collections of these books are found in multiple libraries, calling on the reader to remember the Jews of communities that vanished.

October 7th and its aftermath has brought 1,600 heartbreaking Yizkors to the world. The victims of this massacre and war are disproportionately young, revelers at a music festival, soldiers on the front lines, and Kibbutz families. Over 100 children have been orphaned. In Nir Oz, Tamar and Yonatan Kedem-Siman Tov and their three young children, 6-year-old twin girls Shahar and Arbel, and 4-year-old son Omer, were burned alive in their home, along with Yonatan's mother, Carol Siman Tov. For 1,600 tragedies like this, an ordinary Yizkor no longer suffices.

This Pesach, Rabbi Shlomo Brody published a list naming each person who has fallen since October 7th, along with a new prayer in their memory. This was, as he called it, a time for a "communal memorial prayer." Our congregation found this to be profoundly meaningful. Hopefully, one day someone will be inspired to compose a new *Yizkorbuch*, one dedicated to the memory of those who have fallen in this depraved pogrom.

But even that is not enough.

On the surface, Yizkor is a prayer that makes little sense. Yet its very oddness is the source of its spiritual brilliance, as it is a prayer that makes unique demands of us.

How does one imagine that their acts of charity and prayer here on earth can accrue to the souls of the dead? Some critics dismissed this practice as improper. Abraham Bar Hiyya, a Jewish Philosopher in early 12th-century Spain, criticized the idea as follows:

> "The decrees of the world to come are not conditional and therefore there can be no repentance after death.... the dead know nothing and have no choice between right and wrong. This is why the actions of one's descendants after death can make no difference to the dead man...."

Rabbi Reuven Margolies quotes a similar complaint from an anonymous medieval responsa: "There is no question that good deeds performed for the dead neither help nor save them, for each person is judged according to who they were at death, according to the level of their soul as it leaves their body..."

However, a defense of Yizkor is offered by the Sefer Chasidim. It explains that the past continues to influence the present. If a person educates their children to do good deeds, then even years later those deeds can still be attributed to the parent as well. An act of charity years after someone passes on can still be considered their doing.

This answer still leaves me uneasy. Despite that, it contains a powerful spiritual insight: we must serve as the legacy of those who are gone. Our actions can fulfill their lost dreams. In the Gettysburg Address (which is perhaps the best Yizkor homily ever written), Abraham Lincoln offers precisely this thought:

> "It is for us the living... to be dedicated here to the unfinished work which they who fought here have thus far so nobly advanced. It is ... for us to be here dedicated to the great task remaining before us—that from these honored dead we take increased devotion to that cause for which they gave the last full measure of devotion—that we here highly resolve that these dead shall not have died in vain."

When saying 1,600 Yizkors, we must resolve to do the same. They have left behind much-unfinished work in a terribly imperfect world. And we must vow to carry on their unfinished legacy: to care for their families, rebuild their communities, and ensure that the future of Israel and the Jewish people is brighter than ever before.

In their memory, we must declare: *Am Yisrael Chai*. That is the legacy of 1,600 Yizkors.

Proud Jews, Despite Everything
May 9

Last Shabbat, several synagogues in New York received fake bomb threats by email. These phony messages are called "swatting," and are intended to both provoke a police response and disrupt the synagogues; the emails' IP was located in Finland. At a meeting with the Governor about the incident, one of the rabbis shared with us that her non-Jewish staff members have requested to work remotely; they no longer feel safe coming into the synagogue.

I remarked to the Rabbi afterward: "You don't have to be Jewish to be paranoid about antisemitism."

And there is a lot to be paranoid about. On Monday night, a mass of pro-Palestinian protesters marched up Madison Avenue right outside our building. Some people from our building came out with Israeli flags in response; immediately, one woman had the flag pulled out of her hands and was punched in the side of her head, bruising her eyeball and face.

My neighbor was assaulted because she is a Jew; and this is just one anecdote that reflects the dramatic rise in antisemitism since October 7th. It is not a paranoid anxiety to worry about the safety of American Jews. As Golda Meir famously quipped, "even paranoids have enemies."

History reminds us that we ignore antisemitism at our own risk. Before the Holocaust, too many European Jews missed the warning signs. In 1936, Mordechai Gebirtig wrote a Yiddish poem *Es Brent* (*It's Burning*) in response to the Przytyk pogrom in 1936, where a mob attacked Jewish homes and killed two Jews. The words of the first stanza admonish a lackadaisical Jewish community for ignoring the threats they were facing:

> *It's burning, brothers, it's burning!*
> *Oy, our poor shtetl is burning,*
> *Raging winds are fanning the wild flames*
> *And furiously tearing,*
> *Destroying and scattering everything.*
> *All around, all is burning*
> *And you stand and look just so, you*
> *With folded hands...*
> *And you stand and look just so,*
> *While our shtetl burns.*

By 1939 this poem was seen as prophetic, foreseeing a catastrophe that was about to arrive; Elie Wiesel would later refer to *Es Brent* "as sounding the death knell of the shtetl and a thousand years of Jewish history in Poland."

Some wonder whether America has reached the point of *Es Brent*. While we worry about Israel, visiting Israelis always ask me about antisemitism, uncertain how I can feel safe with all of the mayhem that is occurring here.

Although I understand this fear, I do not subscribe to it. The United States of 2024 is nothing like Poland of 1936. America has a long-standing pluralistic, democratic culture, and American Jews are far from powerless. Most importantly, the vast majority of Americans support us. This is not the time to take flight.

But we can't take it easy either; we must never lose our will to fight. In *The Interpretation of Dreams,* Sigmund Freud recounts a conversation he had with his father Jakob, when he was 10 or 12 years old. Jakob said: "While I was a young man, I was walking one Saturday on a street in the village where you were born; I was handsomely dressed and wore a new fur cap. Along comes a Christian, who knocks my cap into the mud with one blow and shouts: "Jew, get off the sidewalk." "And what did you do?" "I went into the street and picked up the cap." Freud was embarrassed that his father did so little to stand up to an antisemite.

Perhaps Freud's judgment of his father was too harsh; Jakob Freud might not have had much choice in his response that day. But Freud's sentiment is absolutely correct. To hide in the shadows as a meek and weak Jew may be an understandable adaptation to a difficult situation; but left on its own, cowardice will warp the very foundations of Jewish identity. As a perpetual minority, Jews have always been vulnerable to feelings of inferiority that can slowly eat away at the soul. One must be a proud Jew if one is to be a Jew at all.

Rabbi Zadok of Lublin writes that the essence of Judaism is to declare oneself a Jew; everything else is secondary. He proves his point with two texts. One, from the Talmud, implies that a person can convert to Judaism without knowing anything about Judaism. The second, a ruling in the Shulchan Aruch, says that even in times of persecution, it is forbidden for a Jew to claim that they are a non-Jew.

Judaism then is quite simple; to be a Jew means embracing being a Jew, even without fully understanding what that means. And this further implies that all the good deeds and Torah scholarship in the world are not as important as being a proud Jew. (This passage was so controversial, that it was censored out of the initial publication of Rabbi Zadok's writings.)

An earlier precedent goes back to the Tanakh. When Jonah declares "I am a Jew," he is stating all of Judaism on one foot. All the rest is commentary.

Sadly, it's not so easy to be a proud Jew nowadays. The noisy intimidation of poster defacers and encampment makers has driven Jews underground. On the street, kippahs come off and *chai* necklaces are covered up. No one wants to be like my neighbor, the victim of an antisemitic assault.

More insidious is social ostracization, which is far more influential. Students on campus have been frozen out by their friends for refusing to join in protests. Online, Jews on dating apps are peppered with questions about Israel. Appointments are canceled and letters of recommendation denied for having the wrong point of view. Young Jews are now offered the choice to condemn Israel or be considered an enemy of the people; there's no room for conversation.

It is challenging to be a Jew on campuses filled with pro-Hamas professors, activists, and propaganda.

One would have expected students to take the easy route; keep their heads down, go with the flow, and hide their identities. Instead, the opposite has occurred. Remarkably, Jewish students have defiantly declared that they are proud Jews.

In an exceptional letter circulated at Columbia this week, 540 Jewish students (at last count) wrote about their love for Israel. Entitled *In Our Name: A*

Message from Jewish Students at Columbia University, they explained that:

> "Over the past six months, many have spoken in our name...some are our Jewish peers who tokenize themselves by claiming to represent "real Jewish values," and attempt to delegitimize our lived experiences of antisemitism. We are here, writing to you as Jewish students at Columbia University, who are connected to our community and deeply engaged with our culture and history. We would like to speak in our name.
>
> We proudly believe in the Jewish People's right to self-determination in our historic homeland as a fundamental tenet of our Jewish identity. Contrary to what many have tried to sell you – no, Judaism cannot be separated from Israel. Zionism is, simply put, the manifestation of that belief.....
>
> We are proud of Israel. The only democracy in the Middle East, Israel is home to millions of Mizrachi Jews (Jews of Middle Eastern descent), Ashkenazi Jews (Jews of Central and Eastern

European descent), and Ethiopian Jews, as well as millions of Arab Israelis, over one million Muslims, and hundreds of thousands of Christians and Druze. Israel is nothing short of a miracle for the Jewish People and for the Middle East more broadly...

Yet despite the fact that we have been calling out the antisemitism we've been experiencing for months, our concerns have been brushed off and invalidated. So here we are to remind you:

We sounded the alarm on October 12 when many protested against Israel while our friends' and families' dead bodies were still warm.

We recoiled when people screamed "resist by any means necessary," telling us we are "all inbred" and that we "have no culture."

....We felt helpless when we watched students and faculty physically block Jewish students from entering parts of the campus we share, or even when they turned their faces away in silence. This silence is familiar. We will never forget.

One thing is for sure. We will not stop standing up for ourselves. We are proud to be Jews, and we are proud to be Zionists."

This letter is an exceptional statement of Jewish identity, and I urge you to read it in its entirety. Written during a crisis, on a campus filled with contempt for them, they refuse to surrender to ideological bullies who want them to relent and convert to their cause.

These students aren't going to hide who they are. They will not stop standing up for themselves. And they have it exactly right.

They are proud Jews, despite everything. The rest of us must follow their example.

It's Not a Fairy Tale
Yom Ha'Atzmaut / May 16

Israelis agonized over the appropriate way to mark this year's Yom Ha'atzmaut (Independence Day). Thousands of people have lost their loved ones; 132 hostages remain in captivity. Every day is filled with anxiety about the safety of the soldiers and the future of the country. The thought of holding celebrations seems absurd.

However, what is at issue is not just the propriety and etiquette of rejoicing during times of grief. The more significant question is: After October 7th, can we still see Israel as the harbinger of redemption?

Redemption is often seen as a fix-all, the remedy for every problem. But that was never God's plan. Redemption was meant to be combined with reality.

We often forget what the conclusion of the Pesach is meant to be. Pesach is often depicted as an account of liberation from slavery, of the Jews achieving freedom from Pharaoh's oppression. But that is not where the story ends.

Pesach is also the start of Jewish sovereignty. When God declares to Moses that he will redeem the Jews, it ends with the words "I will bring you into the land which I swore to give to Abraham, Isaac, and Jacob, and I will give it to you for a possession." Similarly, the declaration of the bikkurim, made at the farmer's annual offering of first fruits, tells of the slavery in Egypt and then concludes by saying "[God] brought us to this place and gave us this land, a land flowing with milk and honey." Pharaoh's defeat is only the beginning; the Exodus concludes with the Jews being a free people in their own homeland, the land of Zion and Jerusalem.

In Parshat Emor, Pesach has two distinct roles. The first day is a celebration of the Exodus, with the rituals of Pesach sacrifice, Matzah, and the bitter herbs. Then the Bible introduces a ritual for the second day of Pesach: the Omer offering, a simple offering of barley. (This begins a 50-day period of counting days called *Sefirat Ha'Omer*, and on the 50th day is another holiday, Shavuot, on which two loaves of wheat bread are offered.)

With the Omer offering, Pesach shifts its focus to agriculture. Much like Sukkot, Pesach marks both a historical event and an agricultural season. For that reason Pesach is always celebrated during the spring, when the first shoots of barley appear, and the Omer offering is brought in prayer for the crops in the fields.

But why isn't the Omer offering brought on the first day of Pesach? Why is it brought one day after the Pesach Seder?

Another biblical text sheds light on this question. In the Book of Joshua, we are told about the Jews' entrance into the land of Israel, just four days before Pesach. Then the text says:

"On the day after Pesach, on that very day, they ate of the produce of the land, unleavened bread and parched grain. On that same day, when they ate of the produce of the land, the manna ceased. The Israelites got no more manna; that year they ate of the yield of the land of Canaan."

There is a debate on how to interpret this text. Many, like the Rambam, read this as saying that in the days of Joshua, the second day of Pesach is when the Jews first ate from the produce of the land. At that point, they no longer depended on the daily miracle of Manna; they could now take their destiny into their own hands.

Itamar Kislev explains that this is why the Omer is brought specifically on the second day of Pesach. The Omer is both an agricultural and historical ritual; it also was intended, from the moment the commandment was given, to commemorate what would be the first Pesach in Israel, when the Jews first ate the produce of the land of Israel. This was the goal of redemption, and only then was the Exodus complete.

In short, the first day of Pesach commemorates the freedom from slavery, and the second day commemorates the beginnings of sovereignty. The two are inextricably intertwined. Freedom was meant to lead to independence, with the former slaves taking control of their own destiny in their own homeland.

However, sovereignty is not at all simple. Manna, miracle bread from heaven, is effortless, but farming is difficult and uncertain.

This may be why the days of the Omer are seen as tragic. The mourning rituals we practice during the Omer mark the deaths of Rabbi Akiva's students during the Bar Kochva revolt. However, the Kabbalistic view is that the days of the Omer are inherently melancholy, with each day marked by anxiety.

Rabbi Joseph Soloveitchik elaborates on this Kabbalistic sense of dread in his essay *Pesach and the Omer*. He points out that Pesach "represents the transcendental order in Jewish history, or, shall I say, the order of Revelation."

But transcendental experiences must eventually end. As he puts it, "life is full of absurdities and contradictions. There is no longer any revelation... any direct contact with God." In a new land, surrounded by enemies, Israel will have to confront multiple challenges. Nature is not always cooperative, and every harvest is fraught with uncertainty.

The contrast between the miraculous Exodus and the humble barley offering could not be greater. After celebrating a transcendent divine redemption at the Seder, who has any appetite for a grueling, messy, state?

But that is precisely the point. Life is not a fairy tale. Mistakes happen, accidents happen, and eventually, death happens. We don't see God's outstretched arm every day.

The same is true of a country. There will be enemies and wars. Nothing will ever be perfect, and at times, everything will seem to go wrong.

So it is understandable if some wonder whether it is possible to still say Hallel today for a flawed country where the worst massacre of Jews since the Holocaust occurred. Bitterness and cynicism certainly make sense right now.

This is why the second day of Pesach, the day of the Omer, is so significant. The dramatic redemption of the Exodus sets an unattainable standard, one that makes ordinary life seem absurd. But that is the wrong way to look at redemption. Instead, one needs to find transcendence in the humble barley offering.

Farmers labor each year by the sweat of their brow to produce a crop. Some years are successful, and some years are failures. It may seem absurd to continue. Yet the farmer perseveres; and that is heroic. Each year, the first shoots of barley brought in the Omer tells the story of those farmers.

Yom Ha'atzmaut this year resembles the Omer offering—humble, unassuming, and seemingly unworthy of center stage. But like the bowl of barley, what needs to be celebrated right now is not the beauty of what we hold in our hands, but the enormous effort it represents.

Since October 7th, we have seen so many do so much to keep Israel together. Young and not-so-young soldiers picked up at a moment's notice and ran to the battlefield to fight for their country. Everyone else in Israel took care of everything else, from cooking meals, taking in evacuees, and packing gear for soldiers. And Jews from around the world stepped up with advocacy, philanthropy, and volunteering.

This is Israel's Omer offering, humble yet remarkable at the same time.

And that is worth celebrating.

He's Waiting for Us
Bechukotai / May 30

There's a 50-year-old Israeli joke told about Jerusalem's Biblical Zoo, where a remarkable exhibit is mounted about Messianic times. Its centerpiece is a cage with a lion and lamb living together, in fulfillment of Isaiah's vision that "the leopard shall lie down with the young goat." Visitors are amazed by this exhibit; one intrepid reporter decides that he must discover how this is possible. After some inquiries he learns that the zookeeper is none other than Henry Kissinger; and when the reporter finally gets ahold of Kissinger he asks him: "By God, how do you do it?"

Kissinger answers in his trademark monotone: "Every day—a new lamb."

Within the humor of this joke is a commentary on human affairs: those who dream of an otherworldly utopia will eventually find that Kissinger-style realpolitik is inescapable. There are real lions in this world, and one must grapple with them or get eaten alive.

Messianic visions have always stood at the center of Jewish identity; and, in a characteristically overcomplicated Jewish way, there are two intertwined visions. As Avi Ravitsky points out, there are two cataclysms in Biblical history: the exile of the Jews from Israel, and the exile of humanity from the Garden of Eden. Because of this, there are two dreams of redemption from exile. One dream is of a return to the Jewish homeland. But there is a second dream, one very present in Isaiah, of a coming utopia of peace and happiness. And somehow, both visions need to fit into the same jacket at the same time. How that happens is a matter of debate.

The question of what the Messianic period will look like arises at the beginning of Parshat Bechukotai, when the Torah promises that if the Jews fulfill the commandments they will be blessed with peace and abundance. One of the blessings is that God "will remove wild beasts from the land." The meaning of this verse is unclear. Where will all of these animals go? Samuel David Luzzatto, following one opinion in the Sifra, interprets this as a natural outcome of peace and abundance; if the cities are filled with people, there will be no empty buildings or fields that wild animals can inhabit. Of course, wild animals will remain in the forests and jungles.

Others see this verse as being directly tied to the vision of Isaiah. If we are meritorious, nature will change. All of the formerly dangerous animals will be domesticated, and pose no threat anymore.

The Ramban champions this view in his commentary to Bechukotai, where he makes the following claim:

"When (Israel) observes the commandments, the Land of Israel will be like the world was at its beginning before the sin of Adam the first man, when no wild beast or creeping thing would kill a human....It is [because of] this that Scripture says... 'and the lion shall eat straw like the ox'...Scripture stated about the time of the redeemer....that peace will return to the world and all beasts will no longer prey on others and will cease to be dangerous...."

When the Messiah comes, the lion will turn vegetarian. The Biblical Zoo won't have to put a new lamb into its exhibit every day.

The Ramban's view is adopted by the majority of his medieval contemporaries, with one prominent exception: Maimonides.

In his Mishneh Torah, Maimonides makes it clear that there will be no change in nature during the times of the Messiah. He writes that:

"Do not presume that in the Messianic age any aspect of the world's nature will change or there will be a transformation of God's creation. Rather, the world will continue according to its ordinary pattern. When Isaiah states: 'The wolf will dwell with the lamb, the leopard will lie down with the young goat,' they are meant as a metaphor and a parable. The interpretation of the prophecy is as follows: Israel will dwell securely together with the wicked idolaters who are likened to a wolf and a leopard...Similarly, other Messianic prophecies of this nature are metaphors."

Maimonides' view of the Messianic period is consistent with what he maintains elsewhere; that the world always follows the natural order, and miracles, which are few and far between, only occur for significant purposes.

When contrasting the views of the Ramban and Maimonides, one might see the Ramban's view as more distant from our reality. Nature will change during the Messianic period, and God will bring overt miracles to return Israel to its homeland and create a utopian world of peace and holiness. In a dramatic turn of reality, the impossible will come to life.

But actually, Maimonides' view seems even more impossible. If nature is unchanging, history should be stuck in a repetitive cycle of war and peace. After thousands of years of bloody conflicts, how could one imagine otherwise?

Yet Maimonides believes that even if nature cannot change, humanity can. The Messiah, he explains, is a king who will return sovereignty to Israel and teach Israel the ways of the Torah. The Messiah doesn't only battle for a state; he fights to elevate the hearts and souls of his people. Full redemption is only possible when people seek enlightenment and strive to become the best version of themselves.

Sovereignty is the first stage in reaching this utopia. Once people are freed from the pressures of persecution, a revolution of prophetic inspiration can take place. And this inspiration is the very purpose of redemption. Maimonides writes"

> "It is for these reasons, that all Israel, their prophets, and their Sages, have yearned for the Messianic age; so they can rest from the (oppression of) the gentile kingdoms, who do not allow them to rest long enough to properly occupy themselves with Torah and mitzvot. At that time they will find tranquility, and increase their knowledge... In that era, knowledge,

wisdom, and truth will become abundant, as Isaiah (11:9) states, "The earth will be full of the knowledge of God".... And Ezekiel (36:26) states: "I will take away the heart of stone from your flesh and give you a heart of flesh." (The Messiah) will teach the entire nation and instruct them in the path of God. All the nations will come to hear him...."

A return to Zion will allow for a spiritual flourishing that will eventually spread across the globe.

Today, Maimonides' vision of redemption seems further away than ever. Israel was a country divided against itself right before October 7th and may be one again after this war. Dreams of peace seem impossible when pain is all one can think about. Israel endured horrific attacks at the hands of a depraved enemy, leaving a country traumatized. At the same time, one cannot look away from the awful loss of life and suffering in Gaza, which causes profound anguish as well. As Golda Meir said: "Perhaps in time [we will] be able to forgive the Arabs for killing our sons, but it will be harder for us to forgive them for having forced us to kill their sons."

Hopes for universal enlightenment, so common after the fall of the Soviet Union, have gone into reverse. Academic theorists have turned universities into hotbeds of hatred, making Jews the scapegoats for the accumulated sins of Western society, both real and imagined. Social media allows people to find their own "truth," further dividing polarized societies where no one can talk to each other. The dual dreams of the Messianic Age, a return to Israel, and the salvation of mankind, now seem like a bitter illusion.

It would make sense for us to give up on this dream right now. But one must consider that Maimonides' situation was worse than our own. His family fled Muslim persecution in order to remain Jews. Crusaders had ravaged the Jewish community in the Holy Land, and often held Jews there and elsewhere for ransom. Karaites and Rabbanites held an uneasy peace, which often exploded into open conflict.

Yet Maimonides still believed that even without miracles, humanity could change course. He believed that no matter what the circumstances are, the Jewish people can bring redemption.

And we need to take up Maimonides' challenge.

In a sermon given in 1969, Rabbi Norman Lamm related an anecdote told to him by the Israeli General and politician Yigal Allon:

"As a child in his native village near Mt. Tabor, Allon heard the famous Jewish legend about the Messiah sitting in the gates of Rome as a poor leper and waiting. Allon was disturbed by the story, and asked his teacher: "What is the Messiah waiting for?"

The teacher's answer was: "He is waiting for you.""

This is Maimonides' message to us as well.

After October 7th, we must redouble our efforts to both rebuild our homeland and rebuild our souls. Even as redemption seems further away than ever, we must never give up.

We must remember that the Messiah is waiting for us.

Truly Famous
Shavuot / June 6

Each Of Us Has a Name.

This is the title of a poem by the Israeli poet Zelda, published in 1974. This poem had an unanticipated impact; it immediately became part of Holocaust remembrance, and Yad Vashem's project cataloging Holocaust victims was named after this poem. They currently have collected 4,800,000 names. Zelda's poem has been read at multiple Holocaust memorials, and reading the names of victims has become a yearly ritual at Yom HaShoah ceremonies.

The Nazis reduced the Jews in concentration camps to the numbers tattooed on their arms; the purpose of Yad Vashem's project is to reverse that act of dehumanization. The dead are given posthumous dignity, as our community declares that they will not be forgotten.

Anonymity is a curse. To be nameless is to be unloved and rejected. When mentioning the name of a wicked person, the common custom is to add afterward *"yemach shemam v'zichram*—may their name and memory be erased."

It is the names of the Nazi murderers that must be erased, not their victims.

But why are names so significant? As Shakespeare puts it: what's in a name? A name offers no description of the person whatsoever. One could argue it is simply an arbitrary tag assigned to a person at birth, not very different from the numbers on a shipping box.

But that account ignores that as life is lived, each name accumulates new meaning. The Midrash Tanchuma, which served as the inspiration for Zelda's poem, says the following:

> You find that a man is called by three names:
> The name by which his father and mother call him,
> the name by which other men call him,
> and the one he earns for himself;
> and the greatest of them is the one he earns for himself.

Names are not just names. At birth, the name parents give their children is a reflection of the hopes they have for them. Later in life, friends use the very same name differently; it now reflects the person's popularity and status. But ultimately, the name that lasts is earned by good deeds, whether or not others notice.

Names are significant. That is why, when a literary work leaves a character anonymous, it demands our attention.

The Book of Ruth has a character called "Ploni Almoni," which is the rough equivalent to "John

Doe"; it is a term used two other times in Tanakh, and probably derived from the words for hidden and mute. It is the Biblical equivalent of anonymous.

Ploni Almoni is a designated *go'el*, redeemer. His brother Elimelech left Israel to settle in Moab; Elimelech and his two sons died there. Ploni Almoni is obligated to buy back Elimelech's fields and marry Ruth, the Moabite widow of Elimelech's son. By marrying Ruth, Ploni Almoni will be taking part in the ritual of yibbum, and in doing so, continue the name of Elimelech and his family.

When asked to redeem the field, Ploni Almoni initially says yes. When told he must also marry Ruth, Ploni Almoni changes course and says he cannot, "lest I ruin my own estate."

The simple meaning of this phrase is that the financial burden of buying Elimelech's fields will force Ploni Almoni to sell some of his current holdings. But didn't Ploni Almoni agree at first to buy the fields? It seems clear that Ploni Almoni is worried about something else as well.

Seforno offers a different interpretation. He explains that Ploni Almoni didn't want to take a second wife because of the tension it might create in his home. The ruin he is referring to is of his home life.

Rashi offers a third explanation. Ploni Almoni was concerned that marrying Ruth, a Moabite, would ruin his reputation. She was a poor Moabite woman, and marrying her would undermine his lineage.

Both the second and third interpretations are hinted at in the blessings the community gives Boaz after he marries Ruth. In it, they say his house should be like Rachel and Leah's, who are co-wives, and like Tamar's, who is a foreigner. They are telling Boaz he will still be blessed even if the match with Ruth is unconventional, because there is precedent for it working.

Taken together, these commentaries depict Ploni Almoni as a man who carefully maintains his reputation. Some Midrashim say that Ploni's actual name is Tov, which means good. Ploni wants to look good.

But he fails.

Rashi explains that Ploni's name is erased from the Megillah because he refuses to redeem and rebuild Elimelech's family. Yael Ziegler observes that removing Ploni Almoni's name is "an apt punishment, measure for measure, to delete the name of the one who refused to establish the name of his deceased relative."

This, however, is only a partial explanation for Ploni Almoni's erasure from the text; after all, other characters in Tanakh sin, but are not relegated to anonymity. The introduction of this character forces us to consider the larger message of the Book of

Ruth through the introduction of this character, who both plays a central role and is left anonymous.

Ploni Almoni is clearly a man of substance. He is the elder of his family and has substantial wealth, and worries about preserving his reputation and finances. But when it is his time to act, he hesitates instead.

Ruth, on the other hand, is virtually anonymous. She lives with her mother-in-law Naomi, who is old and poor, while Ruth herself is a widow and a Moabite. Ruth lives on the margins, and would be unknown if not for this book.

Even so, Ruth acts with unpretentious kindness and loyalty, the type that doesn't make headlines but that makes a big difference to those around her.

Ordinarily, people focus on the Ploni Almonis and barely notice who Ruth is. And that is why Ploni Almoni is rendered anonymous; the Book of Ruth offers a critique of how we perceive status. The Ploni Almonis imagine that their maneuvers and strategies are of utmost importance, but it is actually Ruth's love that changes the course of history.

That is why the Book is named for Ruth, while Ploni Almoni is explicitly erased. To use the language of the Midrash previously cited, it is not the name that others give you, but rather the name you make for yourself, that counts. And Ruth made a name for herself.

Oftentimes the true heroes stand out of the spotlight. George Elliot expresses this idea beautifully at the end of Middlemarch: "The growing good of the world is.....half owing to the number who lived faithfully a hidden life, and rest in unvisited tombs."

The Book of Ruth throws the spotlight on a woman, Ruth, who lived a hidden life but lived it with extraordinary faith and goodness. It reminds us how much the Jewish people owe her for her quiet heroism.

October 7th could have been much worse. The State of Israel owes its existence to ordinary heroes, who, like Ruth, devoted heart and soul to her survival that day and every day since. (There are also some Ploni Almonis too, perhaps too many.) So many of the heroes are what you would call "ordinary" Israelis, but what they did that day was extraordinary.

Like Ruth, they made their name that day.

Yesterday, there was a brit milah in our community. The baby was named after one of the fallen heroes of October 7th, Chen Nachmias.

The baby's father explained in his speech:

> "Chen was an extended family member of ours who was a magnificent man, father of four wonderful small children,

devoted husband, beloved friend, and a hero of Israel. Chen devoted 25 years of his life to the protection of the State of Israel, including serving in the Duvdevan commando unit, the Shin Bet, and Yamam, which is an elite counter-terrorist unit. On October 7, Chen's unit was called to Sderot, unaware of what they would encounter. He was shot twice and kept fighting until he was literally out of ammunition. He left this world a hero, fighting for the Jewish nation."

And now, thousands of miles away, there is a baby boy that carries Chen's name.

People like Chen are our heroes. They don't need to stand at center stage to make a name for themselves.

To us, they are truly famous. And we will never forget them.

Blood Libels, Then and Now

20th of Sivan / June 27

This past Wednesday was the 20th of Sivan, which was once a fast day that commemorated the first violent blood libel. Later, it was redesignated by the *Vaad Arba Aratzot* to commemorate the Cossack massacres of 1648-1649.

In 1144, twelve-year-old William of Norwich was found murdered. In 1149, a Knight named Simon, on trial for murdering Eleazar, a wealthy Jew to whom he owed money, claimed in his defense that Eleazar and the Jewish community had murdered William as an act of ritual murder.

The defense won the case.

A local monk, Thomas of Monmouth, then published a book about the "murder" of William of Norwich. He made the claim that Jews engage in the ritual murder of Christian children in order to return to Israel. He wrote that:

> "As a proof of the truth and credibility of the matter we now adduce something which we have heard from the lips of Theobald, who was once a Jew, and afterwards a monk. He verily told us that in the ancient writings of his fathers it was written that the Jews, without the shedding of human blood, could neither obtain their freedom, nor could they ever return to their fatherland. Hence it

was laid down by them in ancient times that every year they must sacrifice a Christian in some part of the world to the Most High God in scorn and contempt of Christ, that so they might avenge their sufferings on Him; inasmuch as it was because of Christ's death that they had been shut out from their own country, and were in exile as slaves in a foreign land."

Thomas of Monmouth's blood libel circulated through Europe for nearly two decades; then, in 1171, it became deadly. In Blois, France, a Jew and a Christian brought their horses to drink from the river. The Jew dropped an untanned hide, and the horse of the Christian jumped. The Christian then claimed that the Jew had dropped a murdered baby into the river.

Count Thibault, the local ruler and the brother-in-law of the French King Louis VII, claimed that the Jewish community had committed a ritual murder. The judicial proceedings, which were based on a bizarre trial-by-ordeal, found the Jews guilty, even without a body or an alleged victim.

Thirty-two Jews were burned at the stake.

Rabbeinu Yaakov Tam, the great rabbinic leader and grandson of Rashi, declared the 20th Sivan to be a fast day. He was 71 at the time, and died a few weeks later.

Declaring a new fast for the murdered in Blois was a major statement. No fast had been declared for the First and Second Crusades, which had resulted in thousands of deaths. Rabbeinu Tam himself nearly died in the Second Crusade, but he believed that what happened in Blois was even worse. He recognized that the blood libel was a lethal form of propaganda, one that could cause unending trouble. And he was right.

E.M. Rose wrote an exceptional book on this topic, *The Murder of William of Norwich: The Origins of the Blood Libel in Medieval Europe*. She explains that the blood libel was unique in several ways. First, it was a theory that originated and was embraced by the educated elite, not just the unwashed masses. She writes that:

> "This supposed 'irrational,' 'bizarre,' 'literary trope was the product of lucid, cogent arguments, thoughtfully and carefully debated in executive councils, judged in detail by sober men who were not reacting under pressure to thoughtless mob violence."

The original blood libel started with the intelligentsia; due to their authority, it became accepted as verified truth.

A second element Rose points out is that "Jewish identity was on trial, rather than any single individual perpetrator." The claim made was that Judaism demanded the killing of children; therefore every Jew was now guilty until proven innocent.

The 20th of Sivan has unfortunately become relevant again in 2024. Today, Israel is guilty until proven innocent. Even a hostage rescue is immediately treated as a wanton massacre of innocent civilians until Israel provides video evidence of the contrary.

Once again, leading the charge against Israel are some well-educated people, professors, and students at elite universities, who, in their hatred of Israel, are eager to support a group of fanatical, depraved murderers instead. The testimonies of a handful of Jews, no matter how tainted, are taken to support fantastic falsehoods.

The libel of Jewish ritual murder opened the door to widespread violence. Antisemitism was a noble cause, a way of protecting innocent children. Because they believed absurd lies, medieval antisemites felt justified doing awful things to Jews.

The 20th of Sivan also marks exceptional heroism. The thirty-two Jews who were murdered in

Blois died with their heads held high. Ephraim of Bonn, the great medieval chronicler of antisemitic persecution, writes the following:

> "It was also reported in that letter that as the flames mounted high, the martyrs began to sing in unison a melody that began softly but ended with a full voice. The Christian people came and asked us "What kind of a song is this for we have never heard such a sweet melody?" We knew it well for it was the song: "It is incumbent upon us to praise the Lord of all" (the Aleinu prayer, which on the High Holidays is sung with a special melody)."

These martyrs died while reciting *Aleinu*—they left this world singing a tune from the high holidays.

This is what defiance looks like.

We are the descendants of those Jews. And we too hold our heads high, and defy Hamas and its slandering sycophants.

Yes, It's Our Homeland
August 2

In May, Talia Werber and Steven Goldstein, rabbinical students at the Reconstructionist Rabbinical College, withdrew from the school.

They explained they couldn't tolerate its anti-Zionist atmosphere; of eleven graduating Rabbis, "at least half identify as anti-Zionists or have been participating in anti-Israel protests and actions." Werber and Goldstein felt deeply uncomfortable in an institution filled with "loud anti-Zionist sentiment among the student body and... (a) culture of silence and intimidation that dissuaded students from expressing any positive connection with Israel."

Jewish Anti-Zionism is having a moment. Intellectuals tout the possibilities of "Diasporism," a Jewish identity rooted in exile. A candidate for the Mayor of New York declared at his son's bris that "we are thrilled to pronounce you a Jew without the Right of Return." Anti-Zionist Jewish students are put front and center at campus protests calling for the end of the State of Israel. And at one small Rabbinical School, Zionist students no longer feel at home.

Anti-Zionism is not new. In the 19th and early 20th century, the Reform movement was deeply opposed to Zionism. The Pittsburgh Platform of 1885, which formulated the principles of the American Reform movement, asserted that "We consider ourselves no longer a nation, but a religious community, and therefore expect neither a return to Palestine... nor the restoration of any of the laws concerning the Jewish state."

Early Reformers were deeply concerned with patriotism. After much debate, Jews in Western European countries received equal rights in the mid-19th century. Opponents of Jewish Emancipation argued that the Jews were not loyal to their host countries; because of this, many acculturated Jews bent over backward to prove their patriotism. To be a Zionist then conflicted directly with their desire to be a Frenchman or a German. Which is not all that different than today, when being a Zionist conflicts with being a "true" progressive.

The Reformers hoped they could simply blend in, to be a Jew at home and a German in the street. But then history happened.

By the early 20th century, the world had changed. The turn of the century saw the Dreyfus Trial, *The Protocols of the Elders of Zion*, the Kishinev Massacre, the Beilis Blood Libel, and the rise of antisemitic political parties. In hindsight, all of this antisemitism foreshadowed the Holocaust; one assimilated Jew, Theodore Herzl, saw the handwriting on the wall. He recognized that it was time to seek a safe haven for the Jews.

There is a bitter joke told about a Viennese Jew in 1938, who went to a travel agency to purchase a steamship ticket. "Where to?" the clerk asks. "Let me look at your globe, please," answers the Jew, but every time the Jew suggests a country, the clerk rejects it. "This one requires visa... this one is not admitting any more Jews... the waiting list to get in there is ten years." Finally, the Jew looks up and says: "Pardon me, do you have another globe?"

Jews desperately needed a safe haven in the 1930s, but tragically did not have one.

Israel is now that safe haven. Over the years, she has received Jews escaping from Iraq, Yemen, Syria, Ethiopia, and the Soviet Union. Even today, for Jews in France, Ukraine, Russia, and Venezuela, Israel acts as a security blanket for vulnerable Jewish communities.

However, some young American Jews know little about this history; because they live in an open, multicultural society, they find it easy to dismiss Israel as an anachronism, a safe haven no longer needed. And that is ironic. In the 1940s and 1950s, the argument that Israel is critical for Jewish survival was obvious; but now, that same argument has undermined Zionism in the 21st century. It may be time to look at the larger picture of Zionism.

First, Israel is the holy land of Judaism. The vast majority of the Tanakh is about Israel; Abraham's initial calling from God is to go to Israel. Half of the Mishnah is devoted to laws that are only observed in Israel. Medieval mystics write about the unique spiritual nature of Israel, a land where one is closest to God. The Ramban writes that the mitzvot are designed to be performed in the Holy Land; everywhere else, the performance of the mitzvot is merely a rehearsal.

Israel is also our homeland. When S.Y. Agnon received the Nobel Prize for Literature in 1966, he made the following remark in his speech: "As a result of the historic catastrophe in which Titus of Rome destroyed Jerusalem and Israel was exiled from its land, I was born in one of the cities of the Exile. But always I regarded myself as one who was born in Jerusalem."

This homeland is filled with Jewish history, with a new archeological discovery made every day. The land is filled with Jewish culture, and it is where the Jewish language, Hebrew, is spoken. Many Jews feel immediately at home in Israel.

Israel is a haven, a homeland, and a holy land for the Jewish people. But what makes the story of Israel compelling is something else completely.

During discussions over the possibility of a Jewish homeland under the British mandate, a member of the House of Lords asked Chaim Weizmann: Wouldn't Uganda be just as good?

Weizman responded: "That is like my asking you why you drove twenty miles to visit your mother last Sunday when there are so many old ladies living on your street."

Love connects Jews to Israel. Other places might look the same, but as far as the heart is concerned, they are not at all the same.

Centuries before the phrase "settler colonialism" was invented, Jews kissed the ground upon entering the land of Israel. Rabbi Chiya bar Gamda joyfully rolled in the dust, and Rabbi Abba kissed the stones on the Acre shore. In more recent times, visitors arriving by plane bend down to kiss the tarmac.

Israel and the Jews share a love story that is 3,800 years old. Like all loves, it is an affair of the heart; it has both a hundred good reasons and none whatsoever at the same time. That is why brilliant rabbis swooned like love-struck teenagers when they saw this land.

Some of the most beautiful expressions of this love come from the pen of the medieval philosopher and poet Yehuda Halevi. In one poem he wrote:

My heart is in the east, and I in the uttermost west....

In my eyes it is a simple thing to leave
all the blessings of Spain – for
It is more precious in my eyes to behold
the dust of the desolate sanctuary.

And so he did. As a 65-year-old man, Halevi made the journey from Spain to the land of Israel, despite all the challenges and dangers of 12th-century long-distance travel.

Yehuda Halevi was in love. And so are many young diaspora Jews today.

Young anti-Zionist Jews might grab headlines; after all, the storyline fits the preconceptions of many journalists. But there is a profound love for Israel in the Jewish community, even among its youngest members. Nefesh B'Nefesh, which helps North American Jews make aliyah, had a 120% increase in applications after October 7th. The same has been true in other countries around the world. Despite the increased danger, young Jews around the world feel exactly like Yehuda Halevi.

Audrey, a young woman from Switzerland who was studying at an Israeli university, explained her decision to stay in Israel and make aliyah this way: "When the war broke out people asked me if I was sure I wanted to stay here. Especially since the war I am even more certain. I feel my special connection to the country, and with everything that is happening now, I just can't go back to Switzerland. I feel at home here."

Yes, it's our home, and we love it. That's why we are Zionists.

The Jews Should Have Quit
A Long Time Ago
Tisha B'Av / August 9

After getting tipped off about an impending pogrom, Tevye, the Jewish dairyman at the center of *Fiddler on the Roof*, turns to God and says: "Dear God... I know, I know we are the chosen people. But once in a while, can't you choose someone else?"

Tevye kvetches about the covenant, imagining that a life free of chosenness would give him some peace and quiet.

While this quote is meant as a joke, it still poses a serious question. In times of misery and suffering, why *didn't* the Jews turn their backs on Judaism? Why did they remain loyal to the covenant for 2,000 years of exile? During times of persecution, this question was no joke.

One of the most powerful pieces of Holocaust literature is Zvi Kolitz's short play, *Yosl Rakover Talks to God*. It centers on the last will and testament of the title character, Yosl Rakover, which is recovered from the ruins of the Warsaw Ghetto. Yosl has lost his wife and six children in a series of horrors; now, as he is about to die, Yosl writes a letter to God. At the end of the letter, Yosl cites an account found in Solomon ibn Verga's Shevet Yehudah:

> My rabbi always told the story of a Jew who fled from the Spanish Inquisition with his wife and child, striking out in a

small boat on the stormy sea until he reached a rocky island. A bolt of lightning killed his wife; a storm rose and hurled his son into the sea. Alone, solitary as a stone, naked and barefoot, lashed by the storm and terrified by the thunder and lightning, with disheveled hair and hands outstretched to God, the Jew continued on his way across the desolate, rocky isle, turning to God with the following words:

"God of Israel, I have fled here in order to be able to serve You undisturbed, to follow Your commandments and sanctify Your name. You, however, do everything to make me stop believing in You. Now, lest it occur to You that by imposing these tribulations You will succeed in driving me from the right path, I notify You, my God and the God of my father, that it will not avail you in the least. You may insult me, You may strike me, You may take away all that I cherish and hold dear in the world, You may torture me to death — I will always believe in You, I will always love You! Yea, even in spite of You!"

Rakover continues: "And these are my last words to You, my wrathful God: Nothing will avail You in the least! You have done everything to make me renounce You, to make me lose faith in You, but I die exactly as I have lived, an unshakable believer!"

Kolitz's script is a powerful statement of absolute faith. Although Yosl Rakover is a fictional character, his experience was true to life for many Holocaust survivors. Yes, throughout history some Jews agreed that God should "choose someone else," and cast their lot elsewhere. But like Yosl, most remained loyal to the covenant. And that is remarkable.

Megillat Eicha (the Book of Lamentations) marks the first covenantal crisis, the first time the Jewish people had good reason to exclaim "choose someone else!" The Babylonians had conquered Israel and taken her king captive; destroyed the Temple, the center of Jewish worship; and exiled the Jews. It was an absolute catastrophe on every level. Megillat Eicha is written for these exiles.

Megillat Eicha presents itself as a well-ordered book; four of its five chapters are written alphabetically. But the book's subject matter is very disordered.

There are many different views as to the meaning of the text. Is it an attempt to justify God's judgment by pointing out the sins of the Jews? Is it a protest against God for punishing the Jews so harshly? Or is it merely an attempt to mourn, for the heartbroken to grieve together? Megillat Eicha is difficult to interpret because all of these sentiments, and more, are present within.

Despite its bewildering oscillations in tone, Eicha tells the story of an unchanging covenant between God and the Jews. The Jews are grieving, even angry, but they continue to stick with God.

This was far from obvious. Adele Berlin points out that stylistically Megillat Eicha has a great deal of similarity to Sumerian city laments. However, they are dramatically different theologically. The Sumerians saw the destruction of a city as an end, a time when another city would begin its dominance. Not so, says Megillat Eicha; even in destruction, the covenant remains. Everything else may be disordered in exile; one's thoughts and emotions may constantly change, in confusion and panic. But the covenant remains, from *aleph* to *tav*.

Megillat Eicha tells the story of the first Jews who refused to give up.

Why the Jews stuck with this covenant from catastrophe to catastrophe remains a mystery. Some see the undying faith of the Jewish people as evidence of a divine miracle. Secularists may see it as a response to antisemitism, a defiant stubbornness that refuses to capitulate to hatred. Jewish philosophers might see it as an act of moral heroism; the Jews steadfastly refused to abandon their mission to make the world a better place, despite everything.

Another possibility comes from the very end of Megillat Eicha. After meticulously chronicling the pain and suffering of the destruction, Eicha comes to a close with the words, "Bring us back to you, Lord, that we may return: renew our days as of old." In the midst of destruction, there is a dream of renewal! This can only be seen as Jewish hope, an unwavering willingness to believe in a better future despite the miserable present. We just have to keep moving forward until we get there.

Zechariah refers to the Jewish exiles as *asirei tikvah*, a double entendre that means both "those who are bound to hope" and the "prisoners who continued to hope." Hope defines the Jewish experience, and it has been a consistent source of strength and resilience in difficult times. Hope that we will "renew our days as of old" has kept the covenant alive.

For the last 307 days, we have been a heartbroken people. Like *Megillat Eicha*, contradictory thoughts and emotions jump out all at once. Yet each day the Jewish people return back to the same covenant again and again. And that is because hope is part of our DNA.

Daniel Gordis recently shared an anecdote that speaks to this powerful hope. He wrote that:

> "One of the Shavuot traditions on kibbutzim all over Israel is harvest ceremonies... which includes bringing out all of the new babies born on the kibbutz since the previous Shavuot...
>
> In a video shared on Kibbutz Nir Yitzhak's Instagram page on Erev Shavuot... is the dance of the newborn babies of Kibbutz Nir Yitzhak and Kibbutz Eilot (residents of Nir Yitzhak have been relocated to Eilot since October 7)...
>
> In the video, you'll see a woman wearing a dress and white sneakers. She is Ela Balberman Chaimi, the wife of Tal Chaimi *z"l*. Tal, a third-generation member of the kibbutz, was part of Nir Yitzhak's emergency response team. On October 7, he was taken hostage by Hamas terrorists. It was later confirmed in December that he had been killed on

the 7th and that his body is being held by Hamas.

In May, seven months after her husband was killed, Ela gave birth to their fourth child, Lotan. And here she is, with the rest of the kibbutz, dancing with "the first fruits" of the season..."

Even after such tragedy, Ela and the women of the Kibbutz dance. You might say that maybe they should give up. Maybe they should choose to live elsewhere, maybe they should choose to be something other than Jews.

But they live by a covenant of hope.

And they won't quit.

Backyard Mysticism

Ekev / August 23

"Rabbi Ishmael said: What are the songs that one should recite, one who desires to behold the vision of the divine chariot, and still descend in peace and ascend in peace?"

So begins the book of Hekhalot Rabbati, a mystical work from the 7th century. Spiritual seekers have always craved a direct connection with God, calling out, "My soul thirsts for God, the living God. When will I come to see the face of God!"

In Judaism, this quest is not merely the preoccupation of a few mystics; it is a commandment for all. Parshat Ekev includes the commandment "and to Him you shall cleave" twice; in total, it is found four times in the Book of Deuteronomy. The goal of this commandment, which in Hebrew is referred to as *devekut*, is difficult to interpret. How does one cling to God?

Mystics argue that *devekut* demands an exceptional amount of discipline and effort. Some take this idea to the extreme, and describe it as an experience of *"unio mystica"*, where the person's individuality disappears, and they are united as one with God. But even less dramatic descriptions of *devekut* are distinctly otherworldly. In his commentary on this verse, the Ramban writes:

It is possible that the term "cleaving" includes the obligation that you remember God and His love always, that your thoughts should never be separated from Him...to such a degree that one's conversation with other people is just with their mouth and tongue; yet their heart will not be with the others, but rather with God. With men of such excellence it is possible that even in their lifetime, their souls shall be "bound in the bond of everlasting life," since they have become a dwelling for the Divine Glory....

To cling to God, one must let go of the world.

This vision is both intoxicating and terrifying; the very idea of *devekut* is fraught with questions. How does a lowly being of flesh and blood scale the heights of the divine? And if one visits God's palace, will they care anymore about their own earthly abode?

While it may represent an exhilarating spiritual achievement, the Ramban's description of *devekut* is nonetheless disturbing. The person who succeeds becomes a disembodied soul, a mere shell of a human interacting robotically with others.

In contrast, other commentaries offer more worldly interpretations of *devekut*. Hizkuni says it means to imitate God's attributes of kindness and mercy. The more similar man is to God, the deeper the bond is between them. Rabbi Samson Raphael Hirsch says *devekut* means to be completely devoted to the performance of mitzvot. Rabbi Chaim of Volozhin says that one achieves *devekut* through Torah study. He explains that a person should avoid contemplating the divine worlds while studying Torah because it will impede them from achieving full comprehension of the text in front of them. Instead, he explains that "through deep involvement and rigorous study one cleaves to God's will and words (i.e., the Torah), and God and His will are identical." Cleaving to the Torah is how one cleaves to God.

Similarly, Rabbi Joseph B. Soloveitchik argues that the mystical view of *devekut* "denied man's full selfhood." Quoting the Talmud, he explains that the Halakhic view of *devekut* is that one can cleave to God by "living a life of value and elevation." This perspective is shared by all of the commentaries quoted above. We may never be able to connect to God in a fully satisfying way, but a deep connection to the divine can still be forged through religious and spiritual development.

This "worldly" view of *devekut* is first found in the Sifrei, which says: "How is it possible for a man to ascend the heights and cleave to Him? Is it not written, 'For the Lord your God is a consuming fire'? And 'His throne was like a fiery flame and its wheels like burning fire'? Rather, it means to cleave to the Torah scholars and to their disciples..."

Great teachers are a key link to the tradition, and by attaching to them, a person attaches to the essence of the Torah. And that is why it is a form of *devekut*. Simply being in the presence of great teachers offers implicit lessons about spirituality.

But there is a second element to this text. It locates the connection to the divine in the interpersonal. God is present in the soul of each person, and a deep connection to the divine can be found in day-to-day social interactions.

In a recently published book about Rabbi Yehuda Amital, an anecdote is told about a conversation he had with another Rabbi. Rabbi Amital asked a question on the Sifrei's position — "what if you live in an area that has no Torah scholars?" How would one fulfill the obligation of *devekut*?

The other rabbi responded that if a person has no proximity to Torah scholars, then they would have no choice but to search for a direct connection with God.

Rabbi Amital disagreed. He said if there are no scholars, "connect to a simple Jew. Each Jew is a Torah scroll."

Devekut occurs not just in heaven, but in the classroom as well. And, as Rabbi Amital suggests, *devekut* is possible anywhere another holy human being is found. The spirit of the prophets is found in every caring heart.

This lesson is critical now. In November, I watched a documentary about the Shura army base, which processed the bodies of the 1,200 people murdered on October 7th. A member of the Chevra Kadisha, which is responsible for the ritual preparation of the bodies, related that one of the Rabbis on the base never joined the minyan for prayer services; when he asked the Rabbi why, the Rabbi explained: "I'm not ready to speak to God yet."

In the midst of a horrific war, connecting to God is often impossible. And even though I myself am thousands of miles away from these horrors, my own prayers have suffered as well.

God has stood at a great distance the last eleven months, but at the same time, we have never been closer to Him. We are privileged to be surrounded by remarkable human beings, both in Israel and America, who have done so much: Heroes who leave their families and risk their lives to protect their country. Women who stand alone to keep their families together on the homefront. Remarkable volunteers who work endlessly to help those in need.

All of them ordinary people, all of them ready to act selflessly. They pack backpacks in their homes, and organize fundraisers in their backyards. And when we are with them, we find a connection to the divine that otherwise eludes us.

It is here that one can experience a moment of backyard mysticism, a *devekut* that is possible—even when God seems far away.

Can You Dance with a Broken Heart?
Re'eh / August 29

"Everything seems like it's normal, and that's not normal." In a recent op-ed, Kobi Arielli described the paradox of Israeli life this summer, so abnormal in its normality.

Israel is living a split-screen existence. The beaches are full, the cafes are overflowing, the airport is busy, and the sun shines. That's normal, or at least it should be. But just beneath the surface are constant reminders of how abnormal things are. At Hostage Square in Tel Aviv, art expresses what is too awful for words. In Dizengoff Square, an impromptu memorial for the victims of October 7th rings the iconic fountain at the center. Newspapers regularly have front-page stories about fallen soldiers. There is no longer any separation between mourning and celebration; right now, the time for tears and laughter is uncomfortably jumbled together.

Arielli howls in protest against this strange new reality and concludes that:

> "Life as a whole remains strong and determined. It continues to function, justifiably, in a forced normalcy, out of responsibility for the entire country's existence and out of concern for future generations. But normal? Normal, it is not. Every once in a while, one must

pause, grasp their head firmly with both hands and shout: Noooooo! This is not normal. And it's also not normal that it seems normal."

Israel's communal split-screen existence runs right through the lives of many individuals. Neither shivas nor simchas make appointments; sometimes, they arrive together. Celebrations of every kind, including weddings, bar mitzvahs, and holidays, continue as scheduled, despite the conspicuous void of those who are gone but not forgotten. Widows of fallen soldiers have gotten up from shiva and given birth to babies who will never know their fathers. And then they have to celebrate, because every baby deserves a celebration—but they can only celebrate with tears in their eyes, because they can't help but cry. It's not the way we want things to be. But sometimes, we have no choice.

Grief is untamed, an emotion with a mind of its own. It recreates our perception of reality; C.S. Lewis described it as "an invisible blanket between the world and me." Once grief takes over, nothing else matters.

Intellectuals are at a loss on how to respond to grief. Plato thought grief was an embarrassment for the philosopher, and went so far as to suggest that the laments of great writers be censored so people do not follow their example. He considered grief a cause for shame, best expressed in private. Even Lewis, who wrote a searing autobiographical account of his own grief after his wife's death, refused to publish *A Grief Observed* under his own name or during his own lifetime.

Some rabbis were tempted to see grief as impious as well. In 16th century Egypt, Rabbi David ibn Zimra (Radvaz) was asked his opinion regarding "one of the great rabbis of the generation, whose son died and he did not shed a single tear..."

The Radvaz was shocked by this rabbi's behavior. He explains that it "indicates a hardness of heart and bad character. It is a form of cruelty, and follows the view of the philosophers..." He responds that *Aveilut* (the Jewish mourning practices) clearly demonstrates the spiritual importance of mourning.

At the same time, the Talmud emphasizes one should not mourn excessively. The Ramban locates the source of this idea in Parshat Re'eh, which says, "You are the children of the Lord your God; you shall not cut yourselves nor make a bald spot on the front of your head for the dead. For you are a holy people to the Lord your God..." Mourning must not be expressed by self-mutilation, by cutting one's skin or by tearing out one's hair. One must mourn, but there are limits to mourning too.

Commentaries reflect on the connection between the idea of "you are children of the Lord your God" and the prohibition against self-mutilation. Seforno explains that no matter who has passed away, God, our Father, remains close. Ibn Ezra writes that having faith in God's love allows a person to accept God's judgment, "like small children who do not understand what their father does but nevertheless rely upon him." The Ramban adds that belief in the soul's ascent to God should offer comfort to the bereaved.

Faith tempers grief. Therefore, extreme mourning rituals like self-mutilation have no place among the children of God.

Another perspective on this commandment is offered by Rashi and Shadal. They explain that the children of God must not abuse or abase themselves, even in mourning; they have a higher calling. The obligation of grief must be balanced against the obligation of self-respect. Mourning cannot overwhelm one's dignity.

To grieve is to drown in an unrelenting darkness, each breath too excruciating to take. Everything is but a vanity of vanities, vapid and empty. And it is *precisely here* that the Torah sends us a lifeline, a reminder that we are God's children. No matter what, we must live on. We have too much left to do.

In 2001, Sherri Mandell's 13-year-old son Koby was murdered by terrorists while hiking near her home. In her book *The Blessings of a Broken Heart*, she describes how she was on the day of the funeral: unable to think, to stand, even to breathe. She then recounts what happens when they arrive at the cemetery:

> As I open the car door, Gavi, my six-year-old son says: "I'm hungry. I'm hungry, Mommy."
>
> "What?" I ask. "Didn't anybody feed you?"
>
> "No, I'm hungry," he says.
>
> A policeman makes an emergency run, siren blaring, to a nearby market and brings Gavi potato chips and we remain by the car as he eats. Hunger. Simple hunger. Even at the moment of death. Even at the most tragic, cruelest hour of life, God is pulling me out of my pain by giving me a son who is alive and hungry. God is reminding me that life is all around me, even here, surrounded by dead souls. Gavi is crunching potato chips, enjoying them.
>
> There is a life force that makes us breathe, that calls us to look up to the stars at the most tragic moments. There

is a life force that demands our attention.

Even after a tragic murder, Sherri has other children who need to be taken care of. And in times of grief, the same is true of us; after all, we are God's children, and have no right to neglect ourselves, either. Life continues to call to us, even if we try to shut out her voice.

To live and to grieve at once is to live a paradox. You cry, but then force yourself to smile; you hide away at home, only to be dragged into boisterous celebrations. And yet we must do both.

Don Isaac Abarbanel, in his commentary on this verse, offers an insight into why mourning is an obligation. One explanation he offers is that it is meant "as a kindness to the one who has passed away, to honor them with eulogies and grieving, as the Talmud explains."

We honor the deceased by mourning. At shivas, families put their lives on hold for a week to grieve over a relative's death and contemplate their legacy. The week of mourning publicly expresses that the family deeply misses the person who has passed away. To be mourned and missed is to be loved and respected.

But Abarbanel's explanation offers a missing puzzle piece that resolves the paradox. To mourn honors the dead. But to live on afterward is an even greater honor, because it creates a legacy for those who have passed on.

Rebuilding is an act of love, and it is the only way to carry the past into the future. And it is what Jews have always done.

After the Holocaust, the Joint Distribution Committee took a leading role in helping survivors in Europe. On the lists of ritual objects the Joint distributed are multiple items related to weddings. In October 1946, 822 wedding rings were distributed in the American Zone of Germany. In 1948, 80 *chuppahs* (wedding canopies) were distributed in the Displaced Persons camps in Germany, Austria, Czechoslovakia, and Greece. After years of horror, these young survivors chose life.

And when they had children, they named them after those who had died. Those children became the living legacy of the six million.

Seventy-nine years ago, the survivors of the greatest tragedy in human history confronted a question: Is there room to celebrate when surrounded by tragedy? And they chose to celebrate. They did so because it was the right thing to do, and because it honored those who had passed away.

Since October 7th, the same question has been raised at every Bris, Bar/Bat Mitzvah, and wedding: Can we dance with a broken heart? Yes, we must, therefore we can.

And we will certainly continue to dance in the future, again and again.

Hersh
September 5

He was everyone's Hersh.

Hersh's charismatic smile let you know he was, as his mother Rachel described, a "happy-go-lucky, laid back, good-humored, respectful and curious person." He was, as the death announcement put it, "a child of light, love, and peace." People were drawn to the story of a young man who loved soccer and music, had a passion for geography and travel, who had just gone to six music festivals in Europe over the span of nine weeks.

And then came October 7th. Hersh's last text messages to his family at 8:11 AM were "I love you" and "I'm sorry."

Hamas kidnapped 251 hostages that day. But a statistic doesn't ignite the same passion as an actual person, and through Hersh, the world connected to all of the hostages. Heads of State spoke about Hersh. At the Democratic National Convention, many in the crowd openly wept for Hersh, chanting "bring them home." His image was posted everywhere; "Bring Hersh Home" was graffitied on walls and printed on posters. Tehillim groups prayed for Hersh and a Sefer Torah was written in his merit.

After Hamas murdered Hersh, millions of people cried; they cried for all of the hostages, including the 101 who remain in captivity.

Hersh's story is one of love. His parents Rachel and Jon Goldberg-Polin advocated for him 24/7. Despite their overwhelming pain, what Rachel called "our planet of beyond pain, our planet of no sleep, our planet of despair, our planet of tears," they found the strength to speak out every single day and remind the world how many days it had been since Hersh was first taken captive. Rachel and Jon traveled everywhere to do everything and anything possible to bring him home.

Most of all they told the world how much they loved Hersh and got the world to love Hersh as well. Even at the funeral, in an otherworldly expression of spiritual strength, Rachel declared that "I am so grateful to God, and I want to do hakarat hatov (offer gratitude) and thank God right now, for giving me this magnificent present of my Hersh... For 23 years I was privileged to have this most stunning treasure, to be Hersh's Mama. I'll take it and say thank you. I just wish it had been for longer."

The Rambam says that when you truly love someone, "you will recount their praises and call on other people to love them." And that is what Rachel and Jon did.

Love has its limits. At Hersh's funeral, the speakers apologized to him for being unable to bring him home; sadly, this immense outpouring of love could not accomplish what everyone desperately wanted. But that is not the end of this story. The Song of Songs says "love is as strong as death." Jon declared at the end of his eulogy that Hersh's memory "can begin a revolution." And without question that is what love can do.

Love is belittled because it is bewildering. It is immaterial, a force that needs to be reckoned with but that cannot be measured. Charles Darwin wondered whether altruism would disprove his theory of natural selection; to sacrifice oneself for others contradicts a theory centered on a single-minded pursuit of survival. (A person of faith grappling with the same question would see the traces of a divine love tucked away in the DNA of the universe.) From a political standpoint, love is the frail runner-up to raw power. Machiavelli wrote that, "it would be best to be both loved and feared. But since the two rarely come together, anyone compelled to choose will find greater security in being feared than in being loved." In a world about survival and strength, love is seen as a veneer that covers up far uglier forces.

Judaism takes a very different view and sees love as the very foundation of the universe. There are commandments to love God and to love all of humanity, both the neighbor and the stranger. Hillel explained that the entire Torah can be reduced to the commandment of loving others; one first experiences the divine in interpersonal connections, and only from there does the rest of the Torah become comprehensible.

The world begins with love; the Book of Psalms says "the world was created in kindness." Rav Saadia Gaon and Rabbi Moshe Chaim Luzzatto see love as God's motivation to create the universe. Love becomes the spiritual blueprint for all of existence.

The human love we have for others reflects this larger divine love. Rabbi Abraham Isaac Kook offers a fascinating perspective on Shir HaShirim, the Song of Songs, a biblical book written in the style of a love song. In the Talmud, Rabbi Akiva had already reinterpreted Shir HaShirim as a metaphor for the love between man and God; ordinary love songs don't belong in a holy text.

Rabbi Kook offers a fascinating reinterpretation of Rabbi Akiva, and explains that the ordinary love songs in Shir HaShirim are actually a small-scale reflection of the greater love between man and God; everyday love also offers a glimpse into the Holy of Holies. Rav Kook reminds us that our "ordinary" loves are not ordinary at all. Every true love leads a person to the Divine.

It's difficult to talk about love in a time of war. Yes, love sometimes requires a person to go into battle to protect their family, reluctantly but resolutely. But that is not the goal; Isaiah dreamt of a world where the swords are beaten into plowshares. War is our nightmare; the dream is peace, of each person sitting contentedly under their own vine and their own fig tree.

And that is the love we continue to search for, a transcendent force that will transform history. Rachel explained that Hersh had a unique ability to bring people together and that he had "befriended... German (soccer) fans over the years when they visited Jerusalem to watch their team play soccer. Together they painted a peace mural with both Arab and Jewish residents near our home in Jerusalem..."

We pray for the day when this will be more than a mural.

Jews have always chosen love, even when it is difficult to do so. Machiavelli's approach is tempting; pure strength seems to dominate on the world stage. But it is also mistaken; brute force works for a generation or two, until there is a crisis. Then the fear disappears, and the ruler is deposed. Power is as finite as those who wield it, grasped tightly by princes whose lives are short and temporary.

To survive for a generation or two, one needs power; to survive for millennia, one needs love. And that is the story of Jewish history. Jews are a people who never quit because they had a passion for God, Torah, and the Jewish people. The love Jews around the world had for Hersh (who was named for a great-uncle who had perished in the Holocaust) is part of this same neverending story. The Jewish people are living proof that love outlasts power.

The day of Hersh's funeral, several posts on social media reported about children being named Hersh in the memory of Hersh Goldberg-Polin *z"l*. These were not relatives or even acquaintances of the family. They were just ordinary Jews who cared, who wanted Hersh's legacy to continue onward. They were naming their children after a man they loved but never knew.

They were sharing Rachel and Jon's remarkable love for Hersh with their own families.

And in doing so, they were starting the revolution of love once again.

May Hersh's memory be a blessing, and a revolution.

61643585R00161